SPANISH ARMADA
PRISONERS

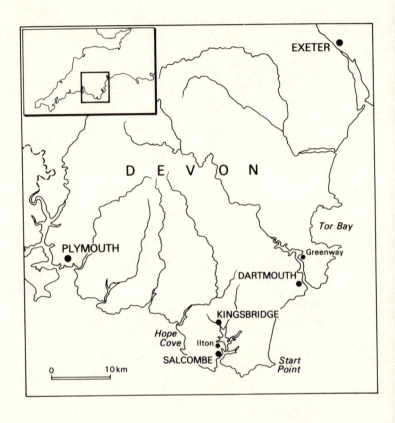

SPANISH ARMADA PRISONERS

The story of
the *Nuestra Señora del Rosario* and her crew,
and of other prisoners in England,
1587–97

by

Paula Martin

EXETER MARITIME STUDIES
NO. 1

EXETER MARITIME STUDIES

General Editor: Stephen Fisher

1. *Spanish Armada Prisoners*. The Story of the *Nuestra Señora del Rosario* and her Crew and Other Prisoners in England 1587–97, by Paula Martin

2. *Lisbon as a Port Town, the British Seaman and other Maritime Themes,* edited by Stephen Fisher (forthcoming summer 1988)

3. *Devon's Coastline and Coastal Waters: Aspects of Man's Relationship with the Sea,* edited by David J. Starkey (forthcoming autumn 1988)

4. *British Privateering Enterprise in the Eighteenth Century,* by David J. Starkey (forthcoming winter 1988–89)

First published 1988 by the University of Exeter

© 1988 Paula Martin

ISBN 0 85989 305 7

Exeter University Publications
Reed Hall
Streatham Drive
Exeter, Devon
EX4 4QR

Designed and Typeset by Scribes, Exeter

Printed and Bound by Short Run Press Limited, Exeter

To my Mother

Contents

LIST OF PLATES viii
PREFACE ix

ABBREVIATIONS AND SOURCES xi

INTRODUCTION:
THE SPANISH ARMADA SAILS 1

1. THE ROSARIO RETIRES FROM THE FRAY . . 6

2. HER CONTENTS AND THEIR DISPOSAL . . 22

3. THE FATE OF HER CREW, AND OF THE MEN
FROM THE SAN SALVADOR AND THE
SAN PEDRO MAYOR 43

4. THE PRISONERS IN LONDON 63

5. DON PEDRO DE VALDÉS 1588–93 79

6. RETROSPECT 90

APPENDIX A:
THE INVENTORY OF THE ROSARIO 98

APPENDIX B:
THE CREW OF THE SAN PEDRO MAYOR . . 100

INDEX 107

List of Plates

Frontispiece   Map of South Devon
Plate 1   Engraving of the capture of the Rosario
Plate 2   Inventory of the Rosario
Plate 3   Engraving of Drake distributing treasure
Plate 4   Spanish bed from the Rosario
Plate 5   'Spanish Barn' at Torquay
Plate 6   View of Exeter in 1587
Plate 7   The Dart Estuary
Plate 8   Hope Cove, South Devon
Plate 9   Portrait of Richard Drake

Preface

THIS TOPIC was suggested to me by Professor Geoffrey Parker, then of St Andrews University and now of the University of Illinois. What began as a straightforward analysis of the inventory made by the English after Sir Francis Drake's capture of the *Rosario* led me into a study which became much broader than either of us had anticipated: a study encompassing the subsequent fate of the ship and her contents; the four and a half years spent in England by her commander, Don Pedro de Valdés, before he was ransomed; and the experiences of the other Armada prisoners in England. To the published sources, mainly in Duro, Herrera Oria, Laughton and the various Calendars of State Papers, I have added other material from the Public Record Office, and a number of Spanish documents, kindly provided by Geoffrey Parker in the form of notes, xeroxes and microfilm.

Wider historical perspectives have been touched on only where they relate to the *Rosario* and the Spanish prisoners. For a recent study of the Armada campaign as a whole see Colin Martin and Geoffrey Parker, *The Spanish Armada* (1988).

I have included a large number of direct quotations (with modernised punctuation and spelling) because I find Elizabethan English subtle, succinct, and expressive. It is, moreover, very easy to misrepresent in precis.

Ducats, escudos, scudi, crowns, pistolets and gold coins all mean the same. There were roughly four to £1. The Castillian *libra* was roughly equivalent to an English pound, and therefore the *quintal* to 100 lbs (a hundredweight: the modern hundredweight of 112 pounds includes an allowance for the container).

All dates are New Style.

Acknowledgements

I would like to thank the following people for the help they have given me. Most of all, I must acknowledge the courteous and patient assistance I have received from the staffs of St Andrews University Library, the National Library of Scotland, the British Library, the Inter-Library Loan Service, and the Public Record Office (Chancery Lane). Messrs Collin Carpenter and Angus Konstam kindly helped with specific points, while Dr Basil Greenhill provided encouragement and advice on publication. Mrs Melva McIntosh generously helped me with translating some of the Spanish documents. Dr Stephen Fisher, General Editor of the Maritime History Series, and the Publications Committee of the University of Exeter have been good enough to accept the work for publication, and I am especially grateful for the friendly help given to me by Professor Joyce Youings, who has provided some of the illustrations, advised on the preparation of the manuscript and, with Mrs Barbara Mennell, the University's Publications Officer, has seen it through the press. The map was drawn by Rodney Fry. My thanks also go to my husband Colin Martin for his constant interest and the use of his own researches. I owe a final debt to Professor Geoffrey Parker, who has been an enthusiastic mentor throughout the past three years.

Crown copyright material in the Public Record Office is reproduced by permission of the Controller of HMSO.

St Andrews 1988   Paula Martin

Abbreviations and Sources

AGS — Archivo General de Simancas:
    CMC — Contaduría Mayor de Cuentas
    CS — Contaduría del Sueldo
    Estado
    GA — Guerra Antigua

APCE — *Acts of the Privy Council of England*, J.R. Dasent, ed.,
    New Series, xvi, 1588 (1897)
        xvii, 1588–89 (Norwich, 1898)
        xviii, 1589–90 (Norwich, 1899)
        xix, 1590 (1899)
        xx, 1590–91 (1900)
        xxiii, 1592 (1901)
        xxv, 1595–96 (1901)

BL — British Library
    Add Mss — Additional Manuscripts
    Lansdowne Mss
    Royal Mss

CSP — *Calendar of State Papers*
    Domestic, Elizabeth, 1581–90, R. Lemon, ed. (1865)
    Domestic, Elizabeth, 1591–94, M.A.E. Green, ed. (1867)
    Domestic, Addenda, 1590–1625, M.A.E. Green, ed. (1872)
    Foreign, Elizabeth, R.B. Wernham, ed.
      XXII, July–December 1588 (1936)
      XXIII, Jan–July 1589 (1950)
    Foreign, List and Analysis
      I, Aug 1589–June 1590 (1964)
      II, July 1590–May 1591 (1969)
      III, June 1591–April 1592 (1980)
      IV, May 1592–June 1593 (1984)
    Ireland, 1588–92, H.C. Hamilton, ed. (1885)
    Spanish, 1587–1603, M.A.S. Hume, ed. (1899)
    Venetian, 1581–91, H.F. Brown, ed. (1894)

Duro — C. Fernández Duro, *La Armada Invencible*, 2 vols (Madrid, 1884–85)

Elliot-Drake — Lady Elizabeth Elliot-Drake, *The Family and Heirs of Sir Francis Drake*, 2 vols (1911)

Hakluyt — Richard Hakluyt, *Voyages and Documents*, J. Hampden, ed. (1965), 358–98. This translation of part of Emanuel Van Meteren's *History of the Low Countries*, written in Latin, was published by Hakluyt in 1598.

Herrera Oria — C. Herrera Oria, *La Armada Invencible* (Valladolid, 1929)

HMC — Historical Manuscripts Commission, Reports

Laughton — J.K. Laughton, *State Papers relating to the defeat of the Spanish Armada*, 2 vols (Navy Records Society, 1894).

PRO — Public Record Office, Chancery Lane, London
    SP — State Papers
        12, Domestic, Elizabeth
        77, Flanders
        78, France
        94, Spain
    E — Exchequer
        133 — Barons' Depositions
        351 — Pipe Office, Declared Accounts

In referring to State Papers, I have given the references used in the PRO. For example, the State Papers Domestic for this period are SP12, the arabic numerals after this are the same as the Roman numerals used in the Calendar of State Papers. Where the papers I refer to have been published in full by Laughton, I have included his reference in brackets.

Ubaldino — *Commentary on the action undertaken against the Kingdom of England by the Catholic King in the Year 1588 . . .* , 'written by Petruccio Ubaldino, Florentine Citizen, in London on the 15th day of April, 1589'. A new translation is in G.B. Naish and D.W. Waters, *The Elizabethan Navy and the Armada of Spain*, National Maritime Museum, Maritime Monographs and Reports 17 (1975), 72–100

INTRODUCTION

The Spanish Armada Sails

This great Galleazzo
  which was so huge and high,
That, like a bulwark on the sea
  did seem to each man's eye.
There was it taken,
  unto our great relief,
And divers nobles, in which train
  Don PEDRO was the chief.
Strong was she stuffed
  with cannons great and small,
And other instruments of war,
  Which we obtained all.
A certain sign
  of good success, we trust:
That GOD will overthrow the rest,
  as he hath done the first.[1]

THUS RUNS a ballad printed on 20 August 1588, before the final fate of the Spanish Armada was known. 'There was a large galleon, commanded by Don Pedro de Valdés, which in tacking fell foul of another and sprung her fore-mast, and was left behind; . . . This ship thus abandoned was taken possession of by Drake. Our chroniclers make a great deal too much of this affair, and, no doubt, more than is strictly true; . . .'[2]

This was written in 1843 by Barrow in his biography of Sir Francis Drake. But historians have continued to discuss the circumstances surrounding the capture of the *Nuestra Señora del Rosario*, and in particular the actions and motives of her commander, Don Pedro de Valdés, and her captor, Sir Francis Drake. The difference of emphasis in the two quotations is the mention of Drake in the later one. At the time, the capture of the

Rosario was seen as important in its own right, and the story was often told without mentioning Drake by name. But later it came to be seen as one of Drake's exploits, and the actual events became overshadowed by his character, or rather the character imputed to him by Victorian and later historians. The capture of the *Rosario* was indeed important, but its importance lay not in the circumstances of the surrender, but in its consequences; the personalities of the individuals involved were much less important. As the result of their actions, however, the Spanish Armada lost its fourth largest ship, one of its squadron commanders, 300 soldiers, about 50 bronze guns, and a large part of the money carried on the fleet. The English, on the other hand, gained firsthand knowledge of the workings of a Spanish ship, and in particular of the defects of her guns and gunnery. They also acquired valuable stocks of powder and shot, of which they were rapidly running short. As well as this, it is possible that Valdés, upset at being abandoned by his commander-in-chief, the Duke of Medina Sidonia, wittingly or unwittingly gave Drake much useful information about the fleet and its intentions.

When the Armada was sighted off Cornwall on 30 July 1588, no one in England had any clear idea of where it was going or what its orders were. War between Spain and England had been inevitable for several years, and it was well known that vast numbers of ships and soldiers were being assembled in Lisbon. Some said that they were to be sent to the Netherlands, finally to defeat the rebels there before Philip II dealt with England; others, seeing the size of the ships involved, thought this force must be aimed at stamping out English piracy in the Caribbean,

> because the Spaniards were deemed not to be men of such small discretion as to adventure those huge and monstrous ships upon the shallow and dangerous channel of England.[3]

(This commentator was right in that the shallowness of the water on the coast of Flanders was one of the factors which would have made the planned link-up between the Spanish fleet and the Army of Flanders so difficult to achieve.) Even if the fleet were being sent to invade England, no one could predict where it was going to land. It was impossible effectively to defend the whole coastline from Cornwall to East Anglia: so the best defence was attack, using the navy to prevent the Armada from landing. As Sir Walter Raleigh wrote in his *History of the World*,

> an army to be transported over the sea, and . . . the [landing] place left to the choice of the invader, . . . cannot be resisted on the coast of England without a fleet to impeach it; . . . except every creek, port, and sandy bay had a powerful army in each of them, to make opposition.

England's best course was to 'employ good ships on the sea and not trust to any intrenchment on the shore,' for

> when those troops lodged on the sea-shores shall be forced to run from place to place in vain after a fleet of ships, they will at length sit down in the midway and leave all at adventure.[4]

Although originally planned to sail in 1587, the Armada did not leave Lisbon until the end of May 1588. And then the weather was so bad and the progress of the fleet so slow that Medina Sidonia decided to put into Corunna to replenish supplies. But when only one third of the fleet had got into the harbour a storm blew up and many of the rest of the ships were scattered. It was nearly a month before the stragglers were reassembled, repairs carried out, and fresh supplies safely aboard. The fleet which finally sighted England on 30 July was, in the words of Sir John Hawkins, one of the English naval commanders, the 'greatest and strongest combination . . . that ever was gathered in Christendom'.[5] It consisted of nine Portuguese royal warships, ten galleons of the Indies Guard (whose usual job was to convoy the annual treasure fleet from the Americas), one Florentine galleon, and 43 large merchant ships embargoed in the ports of Spain and Sicily. These ships were supported by 24 supply hulks and 35 or more small vessels for communications within the fleet and between the fleet and the shore. There were also four great galleasses from Naples, and four galleys, making a total of 130 ships. All four galleys, one of the merchantmen, and two of the hulks failed to reach the Channel. On board this fleet were about 8,000 sailors and over 19,000 soldiers. In addition there were gentlemen adventurers and unattached officers (with their servants), and also gunnery officers, hospital personnel, clergymen, clerical staff, legal officers, and the large personal staff of the Duke. With the rowers of the galleys and galleasses the total came to over 30,000 men.[6]

Against this, the English mustered a fleet of 34 royal ships and 105 merchant ships, supported by 58 victuallers and coasters — a total of 197 ships, carrying 15,925 men.[7]

Philip II's orders to his Captain General of the Ocean Sea, the Duke of Medina Sidonia, were to get his fleet safely through the Channel to rendezvous with the Duke of Parma and the Army of Flanders, and then to escort that army, in its fleet of barges, across the Channel to land in Kent, probably somewhere between Dover and Sandwich. From there the army would march as quickly as possible on London, supported by the fleet in the Thames. At some point during the Armada's advance up the Channel, the English Lord Admiral, Charles Lord Howard of Effingham, realised or found out its intentions, and adapted his tactics accordingly. The vital knowledge that Medina Sidonia did not intend to land in England before his rendezvous with Parma meant that Howard could husband his resources for a few days, and then concentrate on preventing Medina Sidonia and Parma from linking up. It is impossible to determine exactly how and when Howard gained this knowledge, but the capture of the *Rosario* may well have been the reason, or at least the start of the process of reasoning.

Philip II's invasion plans came to nothing. The English did very little damage to the Armada as it sailed up the Channel. But the fireship attack off Calais, when the Spanish ships were 'driven by squibs from their anchors',[8] finally succeeded in breaking the Armada's disciplined formation. Dutch ships were blockading the ports Parma would have to use. The problem of communication between the Army of Flanders and the fleet meant that there would be several days' delay before Parma was ready, and even then he might not be able to break through the Dutch blockade. In the face of the English fleet and adverse winds the Armada could neither wait for Parma nor sail back down the Channel, but was forced to return to Spain round the north of the British Isles.

> Thus the magnificent, huge, and mighty fleet of the Spaniards ... such as sailed not upon the Ocean Sea many hundred years before, in the year 1588 vanished into smoke; to the great confusion and discouragement of the authors thereof.[9]

Notes

1. Thomas Deloney, *A Joyful new Ballad declaring the happy obtaining of the great Galleazzo* . . . (1588), verse 4, reprinted in E. Arber, *An English Garner* (1883), VII, 41.
2. J. Barrow, *The Life, Voyages and Exploits of Admiral Sir Francis Drake, Knt* . . . (1843), 291.
3. Hakluyt, 369.
4. Sir Walter Raleigh, *The History of the World* (1614), extracts reprinted in C. Whitehead, *The Life and Times of Sir Walter Ralegh*, (1854), 56–61.
5. PRO SP12/213/71 (Laughton, I, 361), Hawkins to Walsingham, 10 August 1588.
6. Lisbon Muster, Herrera Oria, 384–433. Some experts mention extra small ships for supply and communications. The hulks which stayed at Corunna were the *David* (one of four carrying pack and draught animals) and the *Casa de Paz Grande*, one of the two hospital ships. The *Santa Ana* (768 tons), the flagship of the Biscayan squadron, was separated from the rest of the fleet in the Bay of Biscay, sheltered at La Hogue, and took no further part in the action.
7. Laughton, II, 324–31.
8. Sir Walter Raleigh, from G. Hammond, ed., *Sir Walter Ralegh, Selected Writings* (1984), 65.
9. Hakluyt, 397.

CHAPTER ONE

The Rosario *Retires from the Fray*

Their force is wonderful great and strong;
and yet we pluck their feathers by little and little.

(Howard to Walsingham, 8 September 1588)[1]

THE STORY of the *Rosario* begins on 20 June 1587, at Cadiz, seven weeks after Drake's famous raid, when she was embargoed on behalf of Philip II for use in the Armada fleet. The *Rosario* was a brand new ship. She had been built at Ribadeo, in Galicia, at the cost of 22,000 ducats, by a partnership of three men, one of whom was Vincente Alvarez, her captain. She had been designed to sail in the *carrera de las indias*, the merchant fleet which carried European goods to the Spanish settlements in the Caribbean and Central America, returning with gold, silver and other valuable cargoes. As soon as she was finished, she was sent to Cadiz for her final fitting-out, and there she was embargoed.[2] She was measured, and her tonnage assessed at 949 9/20 *toneles machos*, which gave her a laden weight of 1,150 *toneladas*.[3] She was to be the fourth largest ship in the fleet.[4]

Gathered in Cadiz bay with the *Rosario* were 19 other similar ships, four galleasses, 12 galleys, 13 small *zabras* and *pataches*, and 30 *urcas* (hulks). The *Rosario* served as the vice-flagship of a group of 15 ships, sometimes called the Andalusian squadron. This group, along with other vessels, under the command of Don Alonso de Leyva, moved to Lisbon, where they arrived on 4 August.[5] There, under the supervision of Don Diego de Alcega, they were made ready for imminent departure for England. Various lists survive of the state of readiness of the various ships, and of things still lacking. The *Rosario* was one of the better prepared ships, despite the damage she sustained to her sterncastle during a storm on 16 November.[6] On 17 November Valdés, who had just returned from America aboard the Indies

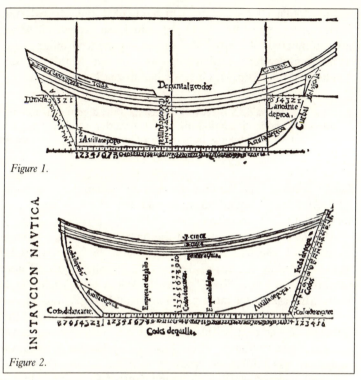

Figures 1 and 2. Typical hull proportions of an Indies Guard warship or galleon (upper picture, bows facing right) and an Indies merchantman or nao such as the Rosario *(lower picture, bows facing left), showing the contrast between the two types.* (From Garcia de Palacio, *Instruction Nautica* [Mexico, 1587].)

Figure 3. Two of a set of seventeenth century playing cards depicting scenes and characters from the Armada campaign. (National Maritime Museum, by kind permission.)

Guard flotilla (the warships which guarded the *carrera*), was appointed to the command of the Andalusian squadron, which now numbered 14 ships.[7] He was an experienced military and naval commander, aged about 48. In the words of one Englishman in Spain who investigated his background,

> I find . . . the said Don Pedro [to] have had the dignities, before this enterprise, both of admiralship and generalship, and to have had much doings touching the building of galleasses and commissions for provision of armies etc.[8]

On 15 January 1588 the final division into squadrons was made. The Andalusian squadron now had ten ships, with a total tonnage of 8,292 *toneladas*.[9]

Although the *Rosario* was not the biggest of the ships brought from Cadiz, she had by far the most and the heaviest bronze guns. According to a list made in July 1587, she carried 51 guns (48 bronze and three iron).[10] In early March 1588 Valdés wrote to the king asking for more guns for the other ships in his squadron,[11] and later in the month he was said to have complained that although he had a sufficient number of guns they were not heavy enough.[12] On 19 March, when inspected by Medina Sidonia, the squadron was said to be ready to sail, but all the ships were reported to be short of sailors and guns.[13] In April Valdés is recorded swapping a *culebrina* for a *medio sacre* with the urca *Duquesa Santa Ana*, presumably trying to sort out the guns in the squadron so that the largest ones were on the largest ships.[14] The final addition of guns to the fleet was documented on 14 May 1588. According to this list, ten guns were added to the *Rosario*; four *medios cañones*, two *cañones pedreros*, and four *falcones pedreros*. Valdés's lobbying had paid off. The Rosario got more extra guns in this final distribution than any other large ship in the fleet.[15] He seems deliberately to have chosen stone-throwing guns, probably because he believed in the traditional technique of closing and boarding in naval fights rather than bombarding the enemy's ships from further away. Stone shot were more effective against people and rigging than ships' hulls. But perhaps he also chose such guns because they were relatively short, and therefore more manoeuvreable on board ship.

As well as her guns and other supplies, the *Rosario* carried a third of the 150,000 escudos carried on the Armada for use in England.[16]

On 30 March the *Rosario*'s crew was listed as 37 officers, 49 sailors, and 31 boys, a total of 117. This number remained fairly constant (Lisbon Muster 118, Corunna 119).[17] She also carried about 300 soldiers: Pedro de Leon and 112 men from the *tercio* (regiment) of Sicily, Alonso de Zayas and 112 men from the *tercio* of Don Agustin Mexia, and Vasco de Mendoza y Silva with 79 men from the *compañias sueltas* (extra, separate companies).[18] According to the published lists she carried no *aventureros* (gentlemen-adventurers); indeed there were only five in the whole squadron, none of whom brought servants with them.[19] This may simply reflect Valdés's personal unpopularity, but it could also be because he had a seamanlike determination not to have his ships cluttered with non-essential personnel. There were, however, seven or eight Englishmen, three or four of whom appeared in the published list of *entretenidos* (unattached officers). This was probably one-third or more of the total number of Englishmen on the fleet and cannot have been chance, but must have been the result of a deliberate choice by both Valdés and the Englishmen. There were no Irishmen on board, although there were a number in the fleet — the English were of more practical use, as it was England where the Armada intended to land.[20] The total number of men on board, therefore, including Pedro de Valdés and his six servants, at least one Spanish unattached officer with his servant, and clergy and medical staff, amounted to a minimum of 443.

The *Rosario* was one of the ships which got safely into Corunna on 19 June, before the storm which dispersed the rest of the fleet. There a council of war was held to discuss whether they should sail for England straight away, or wait for the storm-scattered ships to return, and use the time to carry out repairs and take on more food and water. Almost all the commanders preferred to stay and wait for the stragglers, but Valdés wanted them to set off as soon as possible, arguing that provisions were being used up faster than they could be replaced. He wrote to the King on 5 July recording his dissent.[21] The fact that he had urged the fleet to continue quickly became well known, and changed in the telling to a belief that it was due to Valdés that the fleet had not turned back at this point. According to Marco Antonio Messia, a Genoese living in London who regularly reported to Spain, 'Valdés is disliked by the English, as they say he was the cause of the coming of the Armada from Corunna.'[22]

When the fleet did at last set off from Corunna, it was again scattered by a storm. Valdés gathered his squadron and 40 of the 42 other missing ships off the Scillies, where they were joined by the rest of the fleet on 29 July.[23] The next day there was another council of war. Don Alonso de Leyva, one of the most senior commanders, proposed an attack on Plymouth, where they had just learned that the English fleet was lying. But it was decided not to take such a risk; it was against the King's orders, and the harbour had a narrow and well-defended entrance. Valdés himself, in his subsequent examination, said that he

> was of opinion that it was not fitting to do so, because that the fleet was within the haven, whereof the mouth was so strait as not more than two or three ships could go in abreast, which was insufficient for that action.[24]

While lying off Plymouth, the Spanish ships could see signal beacons or bonfires lit to spread the news of their arrival.[25]

The next day, Sunday 31 July, the Spanish fleet took up its battle-formation, with the *Rosario* and the rest of the Andalusian squadron in the rear of the main battle.[26] The morning was spent in ineffectual shooting by both sides. In Valdés's own words,

> Our ordnance played a long while on both sides, without coming to hand stroke. There was little harm done, because the fight was far off.[27]

Later in the day, however, things began to go wrong. At about four o'clock the *San Salvador*, a 958-ton ship of the Guipuzcoan squadron, was badly damaged by an explosion. Various ships went to her rescue, the fire was put out, the wounded men taken off, and the ship towed to safety in the middle of the fleet. Just before this the *Rosario* had collided with another ship and been damaged. In the confusion following the explosion she suffered another collision which led to quite serious damage. A number of accounts of the incident survive. Valdés's own account was written to Philip II from house-arrest in Esher, a month after the event, and is regarded by some as suspect, because he had had time to choose the wording of his story to show himself in the best light. But the Duke of Medina Sidonia was also trying to justify his actions to Philip II, and although his account was written in the form of a diary, and was sent to the King fairly quickly, it was not therefore necessarily more impartial.

According to Valdés, one of his fellow commanders, Don Juan Martínez de Recalde, who was on board the *San Juan de Portugal*, asked for help because his 'foremast was hurt with a great shot'. But,

> making towards him [Recalde] with my ship . . . it happened that another Biscayan ship of his company, lying so in the way as I [Valdés] could neither pass by nor bear room, on the sudden fell foul in such sort with the prow of mine as she brake her spritsail and crossyard; by reason of which accident, and for want of sail, my ship being not able to steer readily, it happened again that, before I could repair that hurt, another ship fell foul with her likewise in the selfsame manner, and brake her bowsprit, halyards and forecourse.

At this, he sent a message to the Duke, asking that 'he might stay for me until I had put on another forecourse, which I carried spare, and put myself in order'.

> In the meanwhile I got to the fleet as well as I could; and, being to leeward of them, struck the crossyard of my foremast and the rest of my sail, to repair my hurt the better, . . . While I was in this case, the sea did rise in such sort that my ship, having struck sail and wanting her halyard of the foremast, being withal but badly built, did work so extremely as . . . her foremast brake close by the hatches and fell upon the mainmast, so as it was impossible to repair that hurt but in some good space of time. I did again send word thereof two several times to the duke, and discharged three or four great pieces, to the end all the fleet might know what distress I was in . . .

But, he claimed, his pleas for help were ignored, and the Duke sailed on,

> leaving me comfortless in the sight of the whole fleet, the enemy being but a quarter of a league from me; who arrived upon the closing of the day; and although some ships set upon me, I resisted them, and defended myself all that night.

The next day the Spanish fleet was out of sight, and a message being sent from Drake's ship, the *Revenge*,

> that I should yield myself upon assurance of good usage, I went aboard him, upon his word, to treat of the conditions of our yielding, wherein the best conclusion that could be taken was the safety of our lives and courteous entertainment; for performance whereof he gave us his hand and word of a gentleman . . . and I thought good to accept of his offer.

The next day he was taken to see Howard, who confirmed Drake's terms.[28]

Medina Sidonia's account also told of two separate accidents to the *Rosario*, one before the explosion on board the San Salvador, and one afterwards, but then, he claimed, 'The Duke turned to succour him, by giving him a hawser; but though great diligence was used, neither weather nor sea permitted of it'. He was then advised it would be dangerous to wait for her, so he ordered four pinnaces, two ships and a galleass,

> so as to take her in tow and remove her people; but neither the one nor the other was found possible, owing to the heavy sea, the darkness and the weather; and the Duke proceeded on his course, rejoining the fleet and taking care to keep it united . . . This night they removed the wounded and burnt men from the vice-admiral of Oquendo [the *San Salvador*].[29]

This account is very brief, and raises several questions. It is not made clear how long the escort ships stayed by the *Rosario*. From other evidence it would appear that they left before nine o'clock that evening. Although the weather was said to be too bad to take the *Rosario* in tow or get the men off, the *San Salvador* was at the same time safely evacuated.

Another published account is that of Alonso Vanegas, an army captain aboard the *San Martín*. He named the galleass sent to take the *Rosario* in tow as the *Zúñiga*, and said that the attempt failed because the weather worsened, and so the Duke ordered small boats to be sent to evacuate the men and scuttle the ship. But only one boat was sent, and Don Pedro refused to leave his ship unless everyone else could leave with him. Night was falling, and the enemy was approaching, so the *Rosario* and her crew and contents were abandoned by the Spanish fleet.[30]

Those on board the *San Martín* were eye-witnesses of at least some of the action. But we do not know which other ships were near the *Rosario*, and therefore which accounts from those on other ships we should take notice of, and which we should discount as hearsay. Pedro Coco Calderon, the chief purser, was on board one of the hulks. He wrote that after the accident to the *Rosario*,

> Don Pedro fired a gun for aid, and the Duke put about in the direction of the injured flagship, and lay to in order to await her. Don Pedro also lay to, and some ships and two galleasses shortened sail to

help him. But in consequence of the heavy sea they could not venture to send a hawser on board of him. The duke sent two patches to take off the crew, but when they came alongside Don Pedro refused to abandon his ship, as he said he could repair her.[31]

There are a number of other accounts of the incident, some by eye-witnesses, and some previously unpublished, which shed further light on the incident. There is general agreement on the sequence of accidents, and the degree of damage sustained by the *Rosario*. Evan Owen of Esher, giving evidence in a lawsuit in 1605, repeated the story as he had heard it from Don Pedro himself during his captivity.

> Don Pedro thereupon thinking to go to him [Recalde] to relieve him was met by one of the Spanish ships and crossing the same ship had one of his masts struck overboard whereby he was not able to sail so fast and keep company with the Spanish fleet, and [said] that he did send news thereof to the Duke of Medina his general desiring him aid in that distress, but the said Duke did neither stay for him nor send him any aid. And so Sir Francis Drake finding him so distressed did make to him and followed him whereby of necessity he was fain to yield.[32]

Juan Gaietan, one of the prisoners from the *Rosario*, said in his examination on 12 August that the ship was damaged in a collision with another ship of her squadron, and broke her mast(s). He added that Valdés sent some men in a small boat to Medina Sidonia for help, but no reply came. Three hours later, at evening (nightfall?), they were approached by a ship belonging to Sir Walter Raleigh (the *Margaret and John*) which began to fire her guns at her. In the morning, Sir Francis Drake came, and Valdés surrendered the ship to him.[33]

Fray Bernardo de Góngora, who was also on board the *Rosario*, wrote an account of the incident in a letter to a friend. He and 'un cavallero' (probably Pedro de Leon) were sent in a small boat to the *San Martín* to ask for help, because of the seriousness of the damage to the ship. On board the *San Martín*, Diego Flores de Valdés, Don Pedro's cousin, argued that stopping to help would put the rest of the fleet in danger. Medina Sidonia was persuaded: the *Rosario* was left to her fate, and Góngora found himself on the *San Martín* for the rest of the voyage, without any spare clothes. On the northabout journey he was so cold that the Duke lent him one of his cloaks.[34] The Jesuit, Geronimo de la Torre, on another ship, said that two guns were fired, and then a third, to summon help. A Dominican friar (presumably Góngora) and two others left to ask for help. He heard shooting during the night.[35] Juan de Huerta, the paymaster general, was probably not a direct eye-witness as he must have been too busy getting himself and the money off the *San Salvador* to have observed much else that was happening. But he said that one boat was sent to the *San Martín* with two of the 'principal persons' on board, and that a boat was then sent back to ask why the *Rosario* could not follow the fleet. According to Huerta, Don Pedro was surprised, and sent back more people to convince Medina Sidonia of the seriousness of their plight.[36] Pedro Estrade, who was probably on board the *San Marcos*, said that

> . . . about five of the clock in the evening . . . the gallega had her foremast or bowsprit broken. And forthwith she shot off three pieces, but not one of the whole army [*sic*] did come to her. And within a little while after her foremast fell down upon her mainmast; then again she shot off four pieces, but there were none that came to succour her, for that the wind did blow much, the sea was grown, and the English did follow us. At prayer-time we left her . . .[37]

One of the reasons that Valdés's account has been accused of bias is that he did not mention Medina Sidonia's attempts to take the *Rosario* in tow. But although Medina Sidonia and Vanegas made it sound as if an attempt was made but failed, the purser, Calderon, spoke as if no start was made, and none of the other accounts mentioned it at all. Perhaps a tow was in fact ordered to be attempted, but the attempt was abandoned so quickly that no-one on any other ship ever realised what those on board the *San Martín* had planned. As far as those on the *Rosario* were concerned, no attempt was made to help them. Again, only Medina Sidonia, Vanegas, Juan de Huerta and Calderon, all part of the 'establishment', told of a boat or boats going from the *San Martín* to the *Rosario*. Most of the other accounts emphasised the lack of any response from the *San Martín*, and Góngora's unexpected stay on the *San Martín* without any spare clothes seems to confirm this version of events.

The only detailed English account of the incident was the petition made to Walsingham, Elizabeth's Principal Secretary of State, by the captain, master and lieutenant of the *Margaret and John* on 21 August. This stressed the role they had played in the capture of the *Rosario*, in the hope of being given a share of any reward or division of spoils. They claimed that, although the whole English fleet had seen the *Rosario*'s masts break, theirs was the only ship which approached her. They found,

> left by her, for her safeguard, a great galleon, a galleass, and a pinnace . . . all which three, upon the sudden approach of our ship, only forsook Don Pedro, leaving him to the mercy of the sea.

About nine o'clock in the evening they came alongside. Their ship was far too small to attempt to board the *Rosario*, but they

> discharged 25 or 30 muskets into her cagework, at one volley, with arrows and bullet. And presently they gave us two great shot, whereupon we let fly our broadside through her, doing them some hurt . . .

About midnight the English fleet set off in pursuit of the Spaniards, and, fearing Howard's displeasure, the *Margaret and John* joined them. While they were telling Howard their story the next morning, a messenger arrived from Drake with news of Valdés's surrender.[38] This story corroborated what Valdés, Gaietan, and de la Torre said about the shooting during the night, and the Spanish escort ships leaving at nightfall. All these accounts serve to make Don Pedro's story to Philip II much more credible, and to show that there are omissions and bias in Medina Sidonia's own very brief account.

Mattingly, however, in his much-acclaimed *Defeat of the Spanish Armada*, first published in 1959, emphatically condemned Valdés's actions and his version of events.[39] The first point he made was that 'no other account associated Don Pedro with Recalde's rescue. . . . None of the Andalusian squadron was ever near Recalde during the battle'. But although none of the other accounts except Evan Owen's mentioned Valdés going to help Recalde, such an action does make sense. Colin Martin has suggested that the squadrons were administrative rather than fighting units, and that there were certain ships designated as 'troubleshooters', with the freedom to go wherever thay were needed, while the rest of the ships stayed in their rigid formation. This allowed a flexible response to trouble without the fleet losing cohesion. The *Rosario* was almost certainly one of these ships, and it is in such terms that Valdés story of going to help Recalde, and his subsequent manoeuvring amongst other ships, makes sense.[40] The next point made by Mattingly was that Valdés's claim that he collided with a Biscayan ship was inconsistent. But all the accounts agree that there were two collisions, one before the explosion on the *San Salvador*, with a Biscayan ship, and another, in the confusion following the explosion, with the *Santa Catalina*, of his own squadron. (This is complicated by the fact that a Biscayan ship was not necessarily a ship of the Biscayan squadron, but any ship built on the northern coast of Spain, as the *Rosario* herself was.) Mattingly continued,

> Don Pedro says that the duke paid no attention to his distress, but in the next sentence he indicates that the Duke's galleon was near him for some time, and that he sent to it twice.

But this is not at all inconsistent. However close large ships were, help and communication in rough seas involved the use of small boats. Large ships were sent to stand by her, as witnessed by those on board the *Margaret and John*, but the sea was too rough for a tow-line to be attached, so all they could do was stand by to protect her. And they left either because darkness or worsening weather made their continued presence dangerous, or because they were ordered to leave by Medina Sidonia. Mattingly then said,

> The handling of the *Rosario* is the chief excuse for saying that the masters and crews of the Armada were indifferent seamen; the failure to defend her reflects seriously on Spanish courage. For both Don Pedro must be held responsible.

The first point is the question of damage and repair.

> The collision that cost the *Rosario* her bowsprit and the subsequent loss of her foremast may have been unavoidable. But a ship whose bowsprit and foremast have carried away need not remain helpless for more than ten hours . . . with the winds calming and the sea going down it should have been possible to contrive some sort of jury rig . . . and the Rosario, though sluggish, need not have been out of control.

But this is not the point. Before and during repairs the *Rosario* would have been slow-moving or stationary, and difficult to defend, so Valdés wanted his ship to be taken into the safety of the centre of the fleet before he started repairs (as happened in the case of the *San Salvador*), or for the fleet to wait for him while his ship was repaired. So time was wasted while the problem was discussed, and the weather worsened (as all contemporary acccounts agree, despite Mattingly's assertion to the contrary). None of the contemporary accounts, Spanish or English, contains any criticism of Valdés's request. The damage had happened, and it was too bad for the ship to keep up with the rest of the fleet without help.

On the second point, that Valdés should have defended his ship, there was also no contemporary criticism. Valdés did shoot at the *Margaret and John*, which was the only ship which approached him. Her officers admitted that 'by reason of her greatness and the sea being very much grown, we could not lay aboard without spoiling our own ship'.[41] Night fell. Perhaps Valdés should at least have made an attempt to defy any English ship which approached him next morning. But the *Rosario* was too badly damaged to put up much of a fight, and Valdés was cross at being abandoned by his own fleet, especially as it already had one damaged ship, the *San Salvador*, safely in its midst. And so, when he found himself the next morning confronted not by the whole English fleet but by one small boat with a message from Sir Francis Drake offering to negotiate his surrender, he chose, after initial hesitation, to save himself and his men rather than fight, possibly to the death. In the words of Simon Wood, who was on board the galleon *Leicester*,

> . . . after many speeches had of yielding himself, the said Don Pedro answered that he would yield to none but Sir Francis Drake, whereupon Sir Francis Drake sent a boat and took him unto his own ship, who yielded himself a prisoner unto him . . .[42]

And Ubaldino said that,

> Having carefully examined this reply [unconditional surrender or fight] and considering the sad state of his ship, Don Pedro decided to surrender and he took this resolve the quicker when he learned that the man who was taking him prisoner was Sir Francis Drake.[43]

No-one at the time criticised him for this decision.

English accounts differ as to how and why Drake found himself in this advantageous position, separated from the rest of the English fleet. He had been instructed to display his stern lantern, on which the rest of the fleet would keep station during the night. He himself claimed that during the night he had followed some ships, thinking that they were hulks from the Spanish fleet, but they turned out to be German merchantmen. Then he chanced upon the *Rosario*. So he seems to have been on the look-out for spoils, even if the *Rosario* was not his intended victim. This dereliction of duty has worried historians for the last 150 years, as such behaviour does not fit the 'heroic' image of

Drake. Corbett, for example, in his *Drake and the Tudor Navy*, wrote

> . . . it seemed the act of an incorrigible pirate . . . every hour was of importance, and from sheer greed of plunder the great vice-admiral had sacrificed the chance of dealing them [the enemy] a deadly blow for about a day . . . Indeed that a man of his wealth and position at the zenith of his ambition would turn aside at such a moment from the heels of his life-long enemy for the chance of plunder and ransom is quite incredible.[44]

In fact it is exactly what Drake, who was not in fact so very rich, and whose position was dependent on continued success, financial as well as naval, *would* do.

Ubaldino described how,

> Don Pedro surrendered and passed over to Drake's ship with the highest who were with him. And truly he received from Drake no little courtesy . . . Vice-Admiral Drake expressed the wish that Don Pedro should always eat at his table . . . and he desired him to sleep in his cabin.[45]

Other sources agreed with Ubaldino that Drake treated Valdés well. About 40 others went on board the *Revenge* with him, and the money in Valdés's charge was also transferred. Drake ordered the *Rosario* to be taken to shore, in the charge of Captain Jacob Whiddon of the *Roebuck* and 'two gentlemen appointed by Sir Francis Drake'. She was towed to Torbay, presumably the nearest point at the time, and 'the present necessity of her Majesty's service so requiring for the speedy dispatch of the said *Roebuck* again to her Highness's navy', Sir John Gilbert and Mr George Cary, Deputy Lieutenants of Devon, as they reported by letter to Walsingham on 5 August, were asked 'to take the care for the safe harbouring of the said ship.'[46] Torbay was not 'safe harbouring' in the long term, but, as they reported later, she could not be moved immediately, 'wind and weather not serving by the space of three weeks to bring her into safe harbour' in Dartmouth.[47]

Notes

1. PRO SP12/213/64 (Laughton, I, 341).
2. AGS GA 242/86.
3. AGS CMC 2a 1208: C.J.M. Martin, 'Spanish Armada Tonnages', *Mariner's Mirror*, 63 (1977), 365–7. In fact the calculation should have worked out at 1140 *toneladas*, not 1150. But the men who had her built also referred to her tonnage as 1150 (AGS GA 242/86).
4. The largest were *La Regazona*, 1249 *toneladas*, *Santa Ana*, 1200, and *El Gran Grin*, 1160.
5. AGS GA 197/173; *CSP Venetian*, no. 567, p. 305. The other 14 ships were: *Santa Ana* (1200 *toneladas*), *Gran Grin* (1160), *San Bartolome* (976), *San Francisco* (915), *Duquesa Santa Ana* (900), *Concepción* (862), *San Juan* (810), *Santa Catalina* (730), *Santa María del Juncal* (730), *Santa María del Monte Mayor* (709), *Trinidad* (650), *Santa Cruz* (600), *San Juan Gargarin* (569), *La Manuela* (520).
6. AGS CMC 2a 1208; AGS GA 201/272; AGS GA 221/7, 221/43; Herrera Oria, 66.
7. AGS CS 286/1074. The *Santa Ana* had become the flagship of Oquendo's Guipuzcoan squadron.
8. *CSP Foreign1588*, 106–07.
9. AGS CS 278/364. The 10 ships were *Rosario*, *San Bartolome*, *San Francisco*, *Duquesa Santa Ana*, *Concepción*, *San Juan*, *Santa Catalina*, *Santa María del Juncal*, *Trinidad*, *San Juan Gargarin* and the patax *Espiritu Santo*. For comparison:

	ships, total	*toneladas*
Biscayan squadron	10	6420
Guipuzcoan squadron,	9	6194
Levant squadron,	10	8652

10. AGS GA 222/2. Another list, AGS Estado 431/10-11, made at Lisbon on 29 December 1587, gave almost identical figures for the other ships in the group. but said that the *Rosario* had only 25 bronze guns, though these had an average weight of 28.4 quintals, and 18 iron with an average weight of 4.5 quintals. Although the numbers of guns seem wrong, it is significant that the bronze guns are so heavy. For comparison:

	bronze	qtx	av. wt.	iron	qtx	av. wt.
Rosario	25	710	28.4	18	81	4.5
Gran Grin	16	184	11.5	9	92	10.2
San Bartolome	11	159	14.5	16	147	9.2
San Francisco	15	194	13	8	110	13.8

11. AGS GA 222/41, 5 March.
12. Duro, I, 436, 14 March.
13. Duro, I, 442.
14. AGS CMC 2a 1210, 22 April.
15. AGS GA 221/151; in the rest of his squadron, the *San Juan Baptista* got 2 *medios cañones* and the *Concepción* got one. The distribution amongst the other squadrons was:

    Portugal — *San Juan*, 4 *medios cañones*, 4 *cañones pedreros*

    Biscay — *Santa Ana*, 4 *cañones pedreros*, 2 *medios cañones*
      Santiago, 1 *tercio cañon*, 1 *media culebrina*

Levant —*Regazona*, 1 *canon de batir Santa María*, 2 ditto
S María Encoronada, 3 *medias culebrinas*, 2 *canones pedreros*
Valencera, 3 *cañones de batir*
Juliana, 2 ditto

The urcas and the Guipuzcoan squadron got a larger number of smaller guns, perhaps including some redistributed from the larger ships:

Guipuzcoa — 23 new and 15 other bronze guns, 10 iron
Urcas — 8 new and 52 other bronze guns, 25 iron

However, to add to the uncertainty and confusion over gun lists, there is another list of the guns on the *Rosario*. It is the most detailed list we have, but it gives the weight of shot fired rather than the weight of the guns themselves. Its probable date is June 1591. It is so different from previous lists that it is not clear whether or not it includes the final additions listed on 14 May 1588. It is discussed by I.A.A. Thompson, 'Spanish Armada Guns', in *Mariner's Mirror*, 61 (1975), 355–71, and by Colin Martin, 'The Equipment and Fighting Potential of the Spanish Armada', (unpublished PhD thesis, University of St Andrews, 1983), 437.

16. AGS GA 347; AGS CMC 2a 485. The money was divided between 3 ships, the *Rosario*, Recalde's *Santa Ana*, and the *San Salvador*. Of the money on the *Santa Ana*, some was spent at Corunna, some transferred to the *San Martín*, and some off-loaded at Le Havre and sent by letter of exchange to Flanders.
17. AGS CS 2a 272; Lisbon Muster, Herrera Oria, 392; Corunna, Duro, II, 196.
18. Lisbon Muster figures, Herrera Oria, 392, 420–24. Other lists (Corunna, Duro, II, 34–9; AGS CS 2a 278/564) have lower figures, but we know from the names and numbers of prisoners that the Lisbon Muster figures are the correct ones. The only prisoner to mention numbers in his examination was Pedro Martín Cabrito, who said there were three companies of 110 men each (PRO SP12/214/17).
19. Herrera Oria, 406–11. For comparison

Squadron	*Aventureros*	Servants	Total
Portugal	44	247	291 (*San Martín*, 141)
Levant	24	121	145 (*Rata*, 98)
Guipuzcoa	21	56	77 (*Santa Ana*, 66)
Castille	7	16	23
Urcas	10	3	13
Galleasses	3	10	13
Biscay	5	5	10

    The numbers of servants are important as they were all extra mouths to feed and extra bodies taking up valuable space on the ships. The enormous variation in numbers between the squadrons, and between individual ships within the squadrons, is not related to the tonnage of the ship, nor to her man-carrying capacity as measured by the numbers of soldiers aboard. It must reflect a choice by the *aventureros* to accompany certain prestigious people; but these people must have had a veto, so extreme numbers may reflect the vanity of the particular nobleman involved, as well as his popularity.
20. Herrera Oria, 406–18; PRO SP12/214/17–21. The Lisbon Muster included about 7 Irishmen (plus 9 servants) and 11 Englishmen (plus 7 servants). But of the 6 English names from the *Rosario*, only 3 or 4 appear in Duro's list, so we must assume that there were more Englishmen in the fleet than appear in any lists. However, even if his figure is too low, the 7 or 8 on the *Rosario* must represent ⅓, possibly even ½ of the total, including Richard Burley, the best known of the English pensioners in Spain. (See below, pp. 74–6.)

Valdés seems to have gathered intelligence at every opportunity, and may have had quite a well-established spy network. For example, John Donne, an English merchant at Vigo in 1581, went to great lengths to avoid being questioned by the notorious Valdés, hiding 'in a broom close[t] 2 days and 3 nights, without meat and drink'. *CSP Domestic Elizabeth, Addenda* xxvii.1. There were up to 700 English and Irish soldiers, under the command of Sir William Stanley, waiting with Parma's troops in Flanders (Hakluyt *et al.*).

21. AGS GA 225/54; Duro, II, 148–9.
22. *CSP Spanish*, no. 480, p. 483.
23. Alonso Vanegas's account, Duro, II, 371.
24. *Ibid.*, 374; PRO SP12/214/22 (Laughton, II, 28).
25. Fray Bernardo de Góngora, Harvard, Houghton Library, FMS Span. 54, and Medina Sidonia's *diario*. Góngora spoke of fires, Medina Sidonia of fires and smoke-signals. English sources suggest that the official beacon system was never used, but some fires were definitely lit, and were assumed by the Spaniards to be a system of beacons, spreading the news of their arrival.
26. PRO SP12/215/36 (Laughton, II, 134–6); Duro, II, 33; Filippo Pigafetta, *Discorso sopra l'ordinaza del'armata catolica* (Rome, 1588).
27. PRO SP12/215/36 (Laughton, II, 134–6).
28. *Ibid.*
29. Duro, II, 231–2; Herrera Oria, 235; translation in Laughton, II, 357–8. The *San Salvador* was not the vice-admiral of Oquendo's squadron. This is probably a confusion with the other *San Salvador*, which was vice-flagship of the hulks.
30. Alonso Vanegas, in Duro, II, 379–80.
31. *CSP Spanish*, no. 436, p. 441.
32. PRO E133/47/4. For the story behind this lawsuit see Elliot-Drake, I, 80–89.
33. PRO SP12/214/18. The original is in Italian, although Juan Gaietan was a Spaniard. For some reason he was not asked the set questions the other prisoners were, and so he told what had happened to him, adding that Vasco de Mendoza y Silva would corroborate his version of events. (See below, pp. 65–9.)
34. Harvard, Houghton Library, FMS Span. 54.
35. BL Add Mss 20,915, ff. 42–8. Góngora *was* a Dominican.
36. AGS CMC 2a 245.
37. M. Oppenheim, ed., *Naval Tracts of Sir William Monson* (Navy Records Society, XXIII, 1902), 303.
38. PRO SP12/213/89 (Laughton, II, 104–08).
39. G. Mattingly, *The Defeat of the Spanish Armada* (paperback edn, 1970), 244–6, 358.
40. C.J.M. Martin, 'The Equipment and Fighting Potential of the Spanish Armada' *op. cit.*, 66–73.
41. PRO SP12/213/89 (Laughton, II, 106).
42. PRO E133/47/3.
43. Ubaldino, 90.
44. Corbett, *Drake and the Tudor Navy*, II, 230, 232.
45. Ubaldino, 90.
46. PRO SP12/213/42 (Laughton, I, 326).
47. PRO SP12/215/68 (Laughton, II, 190).

CHAPTER TWO

Her Contents and Their Disposal

Watch and look never so narrowly, they will steal and pilfer.

(Cary to Walsingham, 8 August 1588)[1]

ONCE THE SHIP was safely at Dartmouth, the inventory which Gilbert and Cary had promised in their letter of 5 August was made on 7 September and sent to the Privy Council the next day. It was entitled 'the true inventory of all the ordnance, munition, wines and all other things whatsoever . . .'. But apart from guns, empty gun-carriages and some wine, it only listed a few ship's fittings: anchors, cables, sails and 'a great lantern which was in the stern of the ship'. (See below, Appendix A).[2] What else should have been on board?

The Spanish Armada was steeped in bureaucracy, and many of the records survive. But even the lading lists for each ship cannot tell us everything we would like to know. The first list for the *Rosario* was made in Cadiz, and the stores loaded on board may include some items being shipped to Lisbon for use on board other ships in the fleet.[3] Another record was made of goods loaded on board at Lisbon in the first half of 1588. This itemised mainly food (and its associated containers, weights, and measures), and naval and military hardware. It also included various extra supplies which were needed because the fleet took so long to set sail.[4] From the records of other ships we know that further food supplies were added at Corunna, and that there was a certain amount of exchanging of goods between the ships while they waited there.[5] There is also a list of the guns and other weapons added to each ship, to supplement whatever each ship carried when she was embargoed.[6] Despite such an apparent wealth of detail, it is not possible to make an accurate list of the *Rosario*'s contents. There may be overlap between some of these lists, and there may be other lists missing. And, for example, it

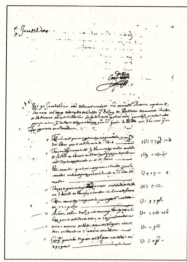

Figure 4. The first page of a list of goods loaded on board the Rosario at Lisbon. The entries include: biscuit, 1,537 qtx 52 lbs (c. 69 tons); wine, 1,901 arrobas (c. 6,650 gallons), in 37 wooden barrels; ... vinegar, 550 arrobas (1,925 gallons), in 20 casks; 222 pieces of bacon weighing 97 qtx (over 4 tons) ... (Archivo General de Simancas, by kind permission.)

is not clear whether the numbers of arms included what belonged to each soldier, or only extras carried as spares or to supply the Army of Flanders. But whatever the exact figures, there would have been, apart from the artillery (see above, p. 8), armour and weapons for the 300 soldiers on board, plus at least some extra extra weapons. There would have been spares for the ship herself, such as rope, canvas, wood and nails. There was food and drink for six months for the 450 or so people on board, and all the associated containers, cooking pots, serving dishes and utensils, and weights and measures. Although some of these smaller items may have been too humble to appear on the English inventory, it is certainly remarkable for its brevity! The only item which can definitely be identified in both a Spanish list and the English inventory is the 'great lantern', which was made of walnut wood, and painted orange and green.[7]

The first goods removed from the ship were the chests of money. As well as any personal monies, there were 50,000 escudos officially on board, in a chest with two keys, one held by the paymaster-general, Juan de Huerta, and one by Valdés.[8] It was common knowledge that this money was on board. When some of the prisoners from the *Rosario* were examined in London, seven of them said that there were 52,000 ducats, two said 50,000, two said 55,000, and one said 50–60,000, adding that the second key was held by Juan de Huerta or Medina Sidonia. Juan Gaietan added that the money was in two sacks within the chest.[9] Valdés, on the other hand, said that there were only 20,000 ducats.[10] Was this a secretarial error? Or could it be that Valdés was trying to cover up for the theft of some of the money, either by his men or by Drake's, during the transfer from the *Rosario* to the *Revenge*, or theft by himself or Drake, or both of them? If so, he overestimated the amount missing, because when Drake finally handed the money over to Howard on 2 September it consisted of 25,300 gold coins.[11]

Juan de Huerta, when he escaped from the burning *San Salvador*, took the money in his charge with him to safety. He later criticised Valdés for not making more effort to send the money in his care to the *San Martín*: after all, he said, it was no great bulk to move.[12] Evan Owen of Esher, interviewed in 1605, said that

> Don Pedro did during the time that he was at Mr Richard Drake's house often speak of many thousands of pounds that was taken in his ship more than he thought that her late Majesty did ever reap benefit by . . .

George Hughes, a witness in the same case, said that

> he was in the ship with Sir Francis Drake in anno 1588 at the taking of Don Pedro de Valdés, and in his ship there was found and taken out a chest of treasure and brought to the said Sir Francis Drake his ship, but before it was brought out of Don Pedro's ship it was broken open . . . between the companies in striving for the taking thereof . . . he verily thinketh and hath heard that some part of the treasure that was in the said chest was embezzzled away as well by Spanish as Englishmen at the time of the entering and taking of the said Don Pedro's ship. . . . [and] he hath heard it reported that the Spaniards when they saw there was no hope of refuge but to be taken or sunk, did pilfer and purloin away out of the said chest much of the same treasure, which he believeth to be true for that he heard likewise that one of the Spaniards that was taken at that time had as much gold about him, as did afterwards pay for his ransom . . .

Hughes also said that the transfer was made in a small boat, the sea was rough, the boat was overloaded, and

> the treasure was brought in the boat in thin canvas bags of which there is great likelihood in such a confusion that some of the treasure was purloined away . . .[13]

Although these accounts were written seventeen years after the event, and in answer to very leading questions, they do agree with the evidence from other sources, and provide extra detail.

Most contemporary commentators assumed that all losses were Sir Francis Drake's responsibility. There was a presumption by at least one observer that money from the *Rosario* had got into general circulation. A newsletter from London reported that 'gold is cheaper here than it ever was'. Spanish pistolets were worth less against silver coins than four months previously (August) 'in consequence of the great abundance of them here. I do not know whether this wealth comes from Cavendish's ship or from that of Don Pedro de Valdés'.[14] Hakluyt, writing not long after the event, said that 'There were in the said ship 55 thousand ducats in ready money of the Spanish King's gold, which the soldiers merrily shared amongst themselves.'[15] And the engraver John Pine, when he republished the Adams charts in 1738, surrounded them with borders of his own design, one of which showed 'Sir Francis Drake, distributing amongst his officers and soldiers, the money etc. that was found in a great Galleon brought to Dartmouth.'[16] The story of fairly open theft of the money, true or not, seems to have lasted until the last century, when it was suppressed as casting an 'unheroic' light on Drake.

According to the prisoners, there were other monies and valuables on board the *Rosario*.[17] Vincente Alvarez, the captain, said that he had brought 4,000 rials (about 400 ducats) of his own, and that others too had money on board. Valdés mentioned 1,000 ducats' worth of silver vessels, while Luis de Ribera said there was 4–5,000 ducats' worth of plate belonging to Don Pedro, and other plate and jewels belonging to the Duke. Most of the prisoners mentioned plate belonging to Valdés or Medina Sidonia or both. Some said there were jewels as well; Alonso Vazquez said there were also pearls, although Alonso de la Serna specifically said there were no jewels. Marcos de Aybar said that the plate was stored in two chests. Vincente Alvarez also mentioned rich clothes, adding that 'he thinketh there was not four ships so rich in the whole armada'. Alonso de la Serna mentioned 'great store of apparel for the Duke of Medina', and Juan Gaietan said there were eight or ten chests containing clothes and other possessions of the Duke and others, and that these chests were taken with the ship, their fate not being known to the prisoners in London. Alonso Vanegas on the *San Martín* also said that some of the Duke's possessions were on board the Rosario.[18]

The chests of valuables seem to have disappeared while the Rosario was being taken to Torbay. In December the Privy

Council wrote to four West Country gentlemen saying that

> by the examination of some of Don Pedro de Valdés' servants it appeareth that there were certain coffers, to the number of fourteen or fifteen, appertaining to the Duke of Medina, wherein was cloth of gold and other rich furniture in the ship wherein the said Don Pedro was taken, which Her Majesty was informed came to the hands of some of those in the Roebuck, a ship belonging to Sir Walter Raleigh, knight, they . . . should send for Jacob Whiddon, captain of the said ship, and examine him and the rest that were in that vessel . . . what they know . . . of the foresaid coffers, and how the same and the stuff and furniture that was in them was conveyed away and purloined, and thereupon to use all good means to recover the same, or so much as may be had . . .[19]

No report survives, and no more was heard of the matter.

Some items that were saved from the ship, because of their symbolic importance, were the flags and banners. The main lading list recorded the provision of one standard of red damask, painted with the royal arms flanked by two angels; a similar one made of linen; linen hangings for the poop, also decorated with the royal arms; and four linen streamers, two painted with pictures of Our Lady, the other two with figures of Christ, and all also bearing the royal arms.[20] On 18 September 1588 there was a sermon of thanksgiving preached at Paul's Cross in London, at which eleven banners were displayed. The most distinctive was a streamer, 'wherein was an image of our Lady, with her son in her arms'. This almost certainly came from the *Rosario*. At the final and most solemn and splendid of the thanksgiving services, which was held in St Paul's on 4 December, a streamer from the Rosario was held over the head of the preacher. The flags were given to St Paul's by Sir Francis Drake, and were lost in the Great Fire.[21]

According to Lady Elliot-Drake, writing in 1911, there was still in the possession of the Drake family a

> carved and gilt bedstead which was removed from de Valdés's cabin . . . It remains in its original condition, or at least as it was at the time when it was taken, for the posts appear to have been shortened about six inches from the bottom, with the object, no doubt, of making the bedstead suitable to the height of the cabin.[22]

This bed still survives (*Plate 4*), with a portrait, reputed to be that of Don Pedro, hanging above it.

When the prisoners from the *Rosario* were interrogated, they gave various figures for the number of guns on board the ship:

40, 42 (40 bronze and two iron), 58 (56 bronze and two iron), and 60. The most detailed account was given by Vincente Alvarez, the captain, who said that there were 58 bronze guns, but seven or eight were taken out before her capture, so there were 50 left, of weights ranging from 75 quintals (7,500 lbs) down to 18. This is almost certainly an exaggeration of the weights.[23] All the accounts, however, agreed that the ship was well and heavily gunned. The discrepancies in the numbers in different accounts can probably be explained by the fact that the smallest guns were hardly bigger than hand-guns, and people varied in the number of such guns which they included in their calculations.

What happened to the guns after the capture of the ship? The inventory, made over a month after her capture, listed 26 bronze guns and two iron ones, of weights ranging from 5230 lbs down to 186.[24] Where were the other 24 or so bronze guns from the ship? One gun had been taken off the ship when she arrived in Torbay, 'for the better furnishing of a ship to join with the navy.'[25] And George Cary admitted that

> there are, I think, 12 or 13 pieces of brass ordnance taken out of the ship, and so left out of our inventory, as your Honour may perceive by the empty carriages which are noted down in the inventory: of the which I take it Jacob Whiddon, captain of the *Roebuck*, had ten.... A pinnace of Plymouth [captain Founes's *Chance*] that came from my Lord Admiral for powder and shot had two other pieces; and the *Samaritan* of Dartmouth had the other.[26]

Were these guns heavy ones, as Lewis argued in his *Armada Guns*, or were they small ones, which were easier to remove from the ship, and more use aboard these smaller ships?[27] Why were the carriages left behind? Was it because they were the old-fashioned Spanish type of sea-carriage, rather than the neater and more efficient type which the English sailors were used to, or was it because the guns were taken for their intrinsic value, and not for immediate use?

Of the rest, the larger pieces were left aboard, but the smaller were taken on shore for safekeeping 'lest that [they] should be embezzled away'.[28] Cary was asked by the Privy Council to get the missing guns back. He asked Jacob Whiddon to return nine (Whiddon said that he had put one ashore at Portland), and Captain Founes (of the *Chance*) to return the two he had.[29] In November the Privy Council ordered the bronze guns, including those taken by the *Roebuck*, to be sent to London by sea. And

Gilbert and Cary were again required to recover the nine guns from Jacob Whiddon, threatening him with prison if he did not comply.[30] In December the Council wrote again, ordering Whiddon to hand over everything he had from the *Rosario* to William Hawkins,[31] a wealthy shipowner and sea-captain, currently mayor of Plymouth, and older brother of Sir John.

On 27 February 1589 the Privy Council wrote to Gilbert requiring him to deliver to Sir John Norris and Drake

> four of the best of the pieces of such kind as they shall think most fit for the service they are to be employed in, with such carriages, sponges, ladles, gynnes and other instruments and necessaries as are and do appertain unto them, and also a convenient number of bullets of each sort remaining there . . . taken also out of the ship of Don Pedro . . .[32]

It appears that Norris and Drake did take up this offer, and that, as the Queen did not in the end provide the siege guns they had asked for, the guns from the *Rosario* were the largest pieces they took with them on their expedition to Portugal in 1589.[33] They attacked the walls of Corunna with 'two demi-cannons and two culverins', but

> let no man think that culverin or demi-cannon can sufficiently batter a defensible rampire: and of these pieces which we had, the better of the demi-cannons at the second shot brake in her carriages, so as the battery was of less force, being but of three pieces.

After the siege of Corunna, they were loaded back on board the ships, and were possibly used again against Cascais.[34] It is not clear whether they ever got back to England, and, if so, what subsequently happened to them.

As for the rest of the guns, in June 1589 the Privy Council sent two men to Plymouth to convey to London various Spanish and Portuguese guns 'as also the ordnance remaining at Plymouth taken out of Don Pedro de Valdés's ship'.[35] In the Chatham dockyard accounts for 1589 is the entry 'for money disbursed for the like freight of the *Richard* of Dartmouth in carrying of seven great pieces of brass ordnance and three bases of brass from Dartmouth to London the sum of £6 10*s*'.[36] It is difficult to trace the guns after this. Over the next twenty years there were a number of inventories made of guns in the Tower of London and on the ships of the Queen's navy. In one list, dated 1595, two of the gun weights tally with guns from the

Rosario, and in one dated 1599 one weight tallies. But the descriptions do not match.[37]

There is an iron gun in Dartmouth which, according to Mr A.C. Carpenter, is of Spanish type; 'The remains of the cast iron gun of 2½ inch bore which . . . dates from the first half of the sixteenth century, might have had association with the Armada. There is no other early gun of this type within 50 miles of Dartmouth'.[38] Unfortunately, it is smaller than the two iron guns in the English inventory, and the prisoners' examinations agree that there were only two iron guns on board.[39]

The English navy's most immediate need was for gunpowder.

> They had not even powder to fire after the combat off the Isle of Wight, until they took that which was on board Don Pedro de Valdés's ship,

wrote Bernadino de Mendoza, the Spanish ambassador in London, to Philip II.[40] By 3 August the Mayor of Weymouth had received instructions from the Council to requisition all Spanish powder and shot for the navy.

> The Right Honourable the Lord Admiral of England, advertising unto me that his Lordship hath taken two great carracks or ships from the enemy, sent to the shore, wherein is great store of powder and shot in either of them . . . requireth that all the said powder and shot be sent unto his Lordship with all possible expedition, for that the state of the realm dependeth upon the present supply of such wants.[41]

But Gilbert and Cary wrote to Walsingham as soon as they took charge of the *Rosario* in Torbay that

> for the better furnishing of her Majesty's navy with munition, we have taken out of the said ship all the shot and powder, and sent the same to her Highness's navy.[42]

How much powder was there on the ship? According to Vincente Alvarez, the ship was supplied with 200 shot per gun, and Diego de Campos, one of the soldiers, said that the ship had 'all other furniture of powder, shot and munition abundantly'.[43] Just before the ship sailed, 1,600 stone and iron shot and over 1,500 lbs of powder were put aboard, to supplement whatever stocks the ship already had.[44] The Privy Council wrote to Gilbert and Cary on 3 August that 'their Lordships are given to understand that there is in the Spanish ship . . . 300 or 400 barrels of powder . . .'.[45] But Gilbert and Cary replied that there 'was in the ship . . . but 88 barrels of powder and 1,600 shot . . .'.[46]

This powder from the *Rosario* had been put to use at once, except for 14 barrels on board the *Samaritan*, which Cary admitted in November had been forgotten and never delivered.[47] The *San Salvador*, too, yielded valuable supplies of powder, so the explosion which damaged her cannot have originated in her main powder magazine.[48]

The list of guns loaded on board the *Rosario* also included, as well as the equipment which came with each gun, one sea carriage, six solid wheels and two field carriage wheels for the guns.[49] In the English inventory there were only two field carriages without wheels, so presumably the spare wheels and the sea carriage had also been 'borrowed' for use on other ships. On the other hand, those who took the 12 or 13 missing guns left their carriages behind.

In Cadiz in July 1587 the *Rosario* was supplied with 150 arquebuses, 30 muskets and 170 pikes.[50] But she may have been transporting these for redistribution at Lisbon. Just before she sailed she was issued with 100 arquebuses, 20 muskets, 300 pikes, six half-pikes, 12 javelins, 24 short spears, and six bill-hooks and cutlasses, as well as shot for the guns, lead for making more, and linen for cartridges.[51] According to some of the prisoners, of the three companies of soldiers aboard, two were armoured, that is, supplied with corselets, pikes and calivers (arquebuses), and one unarmoured, with only calivers and muskets. Juan de Viana said that there were 400 calivers and muskets on board, while Vincente Alvarez listed 150 corselets, 250 pikes, 493 calivers and muskets, and an unspecified number of swords and daggers.[52] It is not clear whether these figures include what each soldier carried, or were all extra supplies. By the time the English inventory was made, nothing was left of all this armament except five sows of lead!

Cary, writing to Walsingham explaining the artillery missing from the inventory, mentioned that Jacob Whiddon also had 'divers muskets and calivers' and the *Samaritan* of Dartmouth had 'ten muskets and ten calivers'. Later he amended this to 12 of each.[53] The rest seem to have disappeared without trace. The Privy Council also knew of armour on board the ship. On 11 September they wrote to the Earl of Bath (Lord Lieutenant of Devon) suggesting that

> such armour as was brought thither in the ship wherein Don Pedro de Valdés was taken might be sold to such persons in the country as shall be willing to buy the same, because there were divers sorts of

armour there of sundry fashions, whereof some were graven and wrought . . .[54]

Either the armour was quickly sold, or it disappeared. The only further mention of armour from the *Rosario* is also the only case where there is definite proof of theft from the *Rosario* while she was still at sea. In 1597 Henry Lake, who had been a seaman on board a Queen's ship in the Armada fight, was found guilty of purloining a suit of gilt armour from the captured ship of Don Pedro de Valdés, of putting it on board the *Minion* of Plymouth, and of subsequently selling it to Sir Francis Drake for £20. It was held to be the property of the Queen, and that he was a common sailor in the Queen's pay. He was ordered to return it or the £20, and to pay costs.[55]

As for the rest of the weapons, Pine, in the decorative borders with which he surrounded his reproductions of the Adams charts, illustrated weapons which he regarded as Armada relics; 'several warlike instruments taken out of the Spanish fleet, and now preserved in the Tower'.[56] But there is no direct tradition of Armada weapons in the Tower. There were Spanish weapons, but it was only in the late seventeenth century that they started being described as from the Armada, and they are much more likely to have come from later Spanish prizes.[57] A survey of ordnance in the Tower of London, dated 1596 or later, listed no arms specifically from the Armada, though it did include Spanish pikes 'armed with velvet'.[58] Ffoulkes, in his *Inventory and Survey of the Armouries of the Tower of London*, reproduced an engraving published in 1791 illustrating an assortment of pikes, maces and similar weapons from the Tower, some of which are labelled as Spanish. The weapons illustrated resemble some of those drawn by Pine, but there is no direct reference to their having been captured during the Armada campaign. Ffoulkes also said that 'it is hardly likely that there were many items from the spoils of the Armada preserved, for a large amount of foreign armour, presumably of Spanish origins, was disposed of in 1588 to provide prize-money for the victors'.[59] As no arms remained in the ship long enough to appear on the inventory, they were probably already in the hands of individuals rather than the state, and their source would not have been advertised.

One of the main concerns of the inventory was the wine. There was no food listed, because what little there was was being used to feed some of the prisoners (see below, p. 44). According to those prisoners they had set out with provision for six months (from Lisbon), or four months (from Corunna). Vincente Alvarez listed 130 or 140 pipes (barrels) of wine (from Jerez, Crete and Rivadavia); ten pipes of vinegar; two pipes of oil; 16 pipes of rice; ten pipes of beef; three pipes of fish; 700 quintals (over 30 tons) of biscuit; three pipes of neats' (ox) tongues and bacon; three calves and 50 sheep. All this, he said, was in the ship when she was taken. According to Pedro Martín Cabrito they had 'sufficient of all thing, except water which was naught and smells'. Others criticised the condition of the food as well as the water.[60] Alvarez's figure of 130–140 pipes of wine fits with the amounts known to be on board.[61] In an explanatory note attached to the inventory, Gilbert and Cary said that the 85 casks of wine, 'were so badly conditioned that they made but 67 full pipes, which are put in safe cellarage; and the wines but indifferent, and many of them eager [sour]'.[62] The same day Cary, writing to Walsingham, mentioned that the *Roebuck* had 'divers pipes of wine and two of oil', and that 'there are four or five pipes of wine and vinegar privily hoisted overboard . . . And so they are not inventoried'. He had also left out of the inventory four pipes of wine, two for himself and two for Sir John Gilbert, and

> if it be not their pleasures to bestow the said two pipes on me, I will pay for them with all my heart as the rest are sold; for in no case . . . would I use any deceit . . . neither will I touch the wines until I hear from your Honour what their Lordships' pleasures are.[63]

Gilbert and Cary's joint letter to the Council also explained that

> we have bestowed four pipes of the said wines: the one on my Lord Edward Seymour [Cary's neighbour, who helped house the prisoners] . . . the other three pipes we gave to three gentlemen that this month have continually lain aboard and attended the said ship. There are also sundry gentlemen and others which have demanded divers pipes of wine heretofore given unto them by the captains, and some of them (as they say) have already paid their money for the same; but yet we have made stay thereof . . .[64]

This implied that some of the purloined wine had been retrieved, or at least traced.

Gilbert and Cary fell out, however, over the safekeeping of the wine, and Cary complained to the Privy Council about Gilbert's laxity. The Council reassured Cary, and ordered Gilbert not to act independently.[65] By mid October even Cary had obviously given up trying to keep track of everything, and hoped that the Council had other things to worry about.

> For the liberal disposing of the wines and other things, it will be over long to trouble your Honours therewith. To be plain, it goeth against my conscience that we cannot yield so just an account of our doings as in duty it appertaineth.[66]

However, he had to keep up his correspondence with the Privy Council because of the prisoners he was responsible for. On 24 October he wrote 'concerning the Spanish goods, I see there is such havoc made thereof that I am ashamed to write what spoils I see'. He had asked Gilbert about the things in his charge, and got no reply, 'but this I know by others, that all the best wines are gone'.[67] By the time the Council decided that the wine should be sold to help pay for the keep of the prisoners, there was little left to sell. In November Cary wrote to the Council that

> money is not to be received for the wines, Sir John Gilbert having disposed already of all the best; the rest, through ill usage in this country, will yield but little, nor good for anything, as I think, save only to make aquavitae of, or such like.[68]

Cary's complaints against Gilbert, and vice versa, were probably not taken too seriously by the authorities; the two men disagreed on other matters as well.[69] No doubt the hope of both the embezzlers and Gilbert and Cary was that after a while the Council would stop trying to pursue the matter, and this seems ultimately to have been the case.

However, when the Privy Council heard of the wreck of the *San Pedro Mayor* in November, they sent down to Devon one of their own clerks, Anthony Ashley, to assist the local authorities to inventory and guard the goods salvaged from the ship. He was also instructed, while he was down there, to investigate the embezzling from the *Rosario*, 'for . . . a great part of the armour, munitions and other things that were in the ship wherein Don Pedro was taken had been embezzled and carried away'.[70] Ashley wrote back to his masters,

> I am put in great hope to discover things of great value which belonged to the ship wherein Don Pedro was, that are embezzled, where, as soon as this business is ended, I will do her Majesty the best service I can.[71]

But he probably did not achieve anything. The last mention by the Privy Council of goods from the *Rosario* was in December, when they wrote to Sir John Gilbert

> to see that the value of the wines disposed of by Hugh Luscombe, his servant, without sufficient warrant, be presently paid over unto Sir Thomas Dennis and Mr Cary, to whom also he shall deliver the rest of the wines and other of the goods of Don Pedro's ship under his charge belonging to her Majesty,

plus any money from anything sold, to be put towards the keep of the prisoners from the ship. If he did not do as he was asked, he would be summoned before the Council to explain his actions. They suggested, however, that Gilbert should be allowed to retain sufficient to reimburse him for what he had spent on the keep of the prisoners.[72]

It is clear from all this correspondence that, because they were captured in war, the contents of the ship, like the money, were regarded as the property of the Queen rather than prizes belonging to their individual captors. However, not everyone seems to have realised that this would be the case. The captain, master and lieutenant of the *Margaret and John* petitioned the Privy Council because, having heard that

> some others besides Sir Francis Drake (to whom the credit and honour of that prize doth most condignly appertain) have made challenge and enjoyed a good portion of the spoil thereof, we have thought good to set down unto Your Honours, in a few articles, the service done by us and our said ship in that behalf; humbly beseeching your Lordships, that if the said prize and prisoners are thought fit to be reparted amongst such as were actors for her apprehension, . . . it may please your Lordships to vouchsafe to peruse our allegation . . .[73]

Unfortunately the Council's response is not on record. On 21 August Martin Frobisher, another of the English squadron commanders, was reported as having said that Drake kept by the *Rosario* all night

> because he would have the spoil. He thinketh to cozen us of our shares of fifteen thousand ducats; but we will have our shares, or I will make him spend the best blood in his belly; . . .[74]

Clearly there was at the time an assumption that all captured ships were prizes. It is not clear why Frobisher referred to 15,000 ducats. Was it a confusion with 50,000, or were there rumours of a specific reward? According to George Hughes in 1605, the money from the *Rosario*

> was delivered by Sir Francis Drake to the Lord Treasurer to her late Majesty's use, but after that the Lord Admiral and Sir Francis Drake and others were authorised by the late Queen to bestow some of the same treasure upon the commanders gents and others that were in that voyage, whereof this deponent had a part.

But Evan Owen said

> that the said Sir Francis Drake had given £2,000 to two commanders that served in the said fleet in anno domini 1588, and . . . £100 unto him [and] . . . Richard Drake for their secrecy therein.[75]

Drake's own account book recorded the payment of £110 'given in reward to the company of the *Revenge* after the second day's fighting'.[76] It is not clear from these sources whether such distribution of money from the *Rosario* as took place was official or unofficial, or both. However, Drake himself did have enough money, presumably from the capture of the *Rosario*, to enable him, in February 1589, to buy a London house. The Herbar, in Dowgate, was a recently rebuilt and modernized house fronting the Thames, next door to the Steelyard, the headquarters of the Hanseatic League in London. He sold it to finance his last expedition.[77]

When Gilbert and Cary sent the inventory of the *Rosario* to the Privy Council, they included a list of the expenses they had incurred so far. These included £1 9s 4d to set up the jury mast at Torbay, and £1 6s 9d for eight boats to tow the ship from Torbay to Dartmouth. The total cost for 'the guarding of Don Pedro's ship in Torbay and for the unloading of the goods within' came to £84 8s 11d.[78] After the inventory had been taken, there seems to have been little or no interest shown in the ship herself. On 24 October Cary complained to the Privy Council that

> the tackle of the ship [is] so spoiled by his [Gilbert's] negligent looking unto, that £200 in ropes and other necessaries will not suffice to set her to the seas again.[79]

In late November there was a rumour in Spain that the ship had sunk while being towed to Dover. But this was probably a confusion with the *San Salvador*, which sank in Studland Bay while being towed from Weymouth to Portsmouth.[80] As we have seen, Drake and Norris accepted the Queen's offer of the four best guns from the *Rosario* for their expedition to Portugal. But although Antonio de Vega, in his newsletter from London to Spain, reporting the preparations for the Portugal expedition, did say 'they are also repairing the Indian ship [*San Felipe*] and that of Don Pedro de Valdés', implying that both were to be used on the expedition, there is no definite evidence that Drake and Norris ever were offered or asked for the use of the *Rosario*.[81]

In May 1589 the Privy Council required Sir John Gilbert

> to deliver the said ship, with all the tackle, munition, ordnance and other furniture thereto belonging . . . to the said William Hawkins . . . [and] the Spaniards who were best acquainted with the air of the vessel should cleans and make her as sweet as could be possibly.[82]

But it seems that she was not actually moved to Plymouth, just transferred to a different custodian. It was not made clear why this was done, though it may well have been because of Sir John Gilbert's neglect of the ship.[83] Hawkins was instructed to prepare the ship to be moved to London. In late June the Privy Council wrote to the Earl of Bath

> . . . touching the powder which remaineth in her Majesty's store in that county [Devon] we pray your Lordship to give order that the same may forthwith be conveyed to the Spanish carrack at Dartmouth wherein Don Pedro arrived, to be brought up to London . . . [unless] perchance the said carrack shall be departed from thence towards the city of London according to appointment from us . . .[84]

From the Chatham dockyard accounts we know that the *Rosario* was at sea from 8 July to 5 August 1589, after four weeks spent preparing her for the journey. The cost of 'transporting the ship lately Don Pedro's from Dartmouth to Chatham', paying 121 men for some or all of the time at the rate of 14 shillings per month, plus their food while at sea, came to £168. As well as this, £22 13*s* 2*d* was paid to

> Christopher Chapman, John Hawkins and ten other shipcarpenters working upon the ransacking, caulking, and dubbing the ship lately Don Pedro's against her transporting from Dartmouth to Chatham, finding at their own charges all manner of stuff and workmanship.

Sometime later in 1589 the *Rosario* was moved from Chatham to Deptford to be dry docked.[85] In a list of the navy made in December 1589 'Don Pedro's ship' is written (in a different hand to the rest of the document) beside 'some merchant ships for victuallers of 200 tonne'.[86] In 1591 she appeared at the end of a list of 25 ships to stay at Chatham.[87] According to Oppenheim, the *Rosario* was on the effective list until 1594.[88]

She met an undignified end. In 1618 the Chatham dockyard accounts recorded that

> Thomas Wood shipwright and sundry others . . . in digging out the old Spanish ship at Chatham near the galley dock and clearing her of all the slubb, ballast and other trash within board, making her swim and removing her near unto the mast dock where she was laid and sunk for the defence and preservation of the wharf there,

were paid at 16*d* per day, for 827 days between them, a total cost of £55 3*s* 11*d*.

> And for hire of lighters with their men for their carrying away all the carts of slubb and other trash which was digged and caste out of the said old ship

at the same rate of pay, for 118 days, amounting to £7 17*s* 4*d*; a grand total of £63 1*s* 3*d*.[89] Finally, in 1622, a payment of £8 7*s* was made to

> Thomas Wood shipwright for breaking up and carrying away the hull of the ship called Don Pedro and two old sunken long boats that lay as impediments of the wharves near the new dockyard . . .[90]

Why was one of the finest of the ships of the Spanish Armada never used by the English? First of all, while the prisoners and the contents of the ship were being sorted out, the ship herself was neglected, until she needed a lot of work done on her before she was ready to sail up the Channel to Chatham. But even when repaired she was not in fact very useful. She was not a warship, but a large armed merchantman. Nor could she be converted to a warship. The Armada campaign had proved the worth of the new design of English warship, finer-lined and faster-sailing than their taller and heavier Spanish opponents. An old-fashioned Spanish ship was of no use except as a merchantman. So the *Rosario* was put among the supply ships. It seems likely, however, that she was never used as such. She was probably less suitable than the much smaller ships normally used for this purpose. Was she, from 1594 to 1618, a tourist attraction, as the *Golden Hind* was before her, and the *Victory* and other fine ships still are today? Or was she quickly forgotten, and left to rot?

Notes

1. PRO SP12/215/67 (Laughton, II, 187).
2. PRO SP12/215/67i, 68 (Laughton, II, 188–92).
3. AGS CS 2a 274, San Lúcar de Barrameda, 12 July 1587.
4. AGS CMC 2a 1012, Lisbon, 17 February and 23 April—24 May 1588.
5. For example, AGS CS 2a 280/1480 (*La Trinidad Valencera*), 280/1937 (*El Gran Grifón*).
6. AGS GA 221/151.
7. PRO SP12/215/67.i; AGS CMC 2a 1012.
8. AGS CMC 2a 485.[9] PRO SP12/214/17, 18, 19.
10. PRO SP12/214/22 (Laughton, II, 27–9).
    The original is in Spanish, but not in Valdés's own writing. The number is clearly *veynte*.
11. PRO SP12/215/59, 59.i (Laughton, II, 167–9).
12. AGS CMC 2a 485.
13. PRO E133/47/4.
14. *CSP Spanish*, no. 481, pp. 491–2.
15. Hakluyt, 377.
16. J. Pine, *The Tapestry Hangings in the House of Lords; representing several engagements between the English and Spanish fleets in . . . 1588 . . .*, (2nd edn 1753).
17. PRO SP12/214/17, 18, 19, 22. See below, pp. 67–9, for details of these men.
18. Duro, II, 380.
19. *APCE*, xvi, 363, 11 December. The gentlemen were Peter Edgecombe, Richard Champernown, Hugh Fortescue, and Christopher Harris. Perhaps the fact that Raleigh, the owner of the *Roebuck* was Sir John Gilbert's half-brother, meant that he was allowed to get away with more than some other people. There is a copy of a letter from Raleigh to Gilbert (23 September 1988) concerning the sale of wine, presumably from the *Rosario* (PRO SP9/55).
20. AGS CMC 2a 1012.
21. *CSP Dom. 1581–90*, 536; Nichols, *The Progresses of Queen Elizabeth* (1823), II, 537–42; Elliot-Drake, I, 105; Ubaldino 100. Also *CSP Span.*, no. 437, p. 438, 'A fortnight ago they placed in St Paul's the banners they took from Valdés' ship and the galleass (*San Lorenzo*). There are also 4 infantry standards, and some other flags and banners. They say that one of the flags is the cross of Burgundy, quartered with the arms of France and the rose of England. This gives rise to much talk here, the said banners having been kept on deck for everyone to see.'

    And according to Robert Greene, *The Spanish Masquerado* (1589), motto 9, 'in the one [of his Ensigns, Banners and Streamers] was figured a Sun and a Moon, the Motto in Spanish, but to this effect *Heri plenilunium, hodie defectus* Yesterday the Full, but to day the Wane: meaning (as I suppose) that the fullness of England's prosperity was at an end, and now by his means should it fall into the Wane: on the other side was depainted an Altar with sacrifice fuming, the Poesie: *sic cupio, sic cogito: spiritus ab inquietudine coactus*: I cannot well discourse his meaning in this: but no doubt whatsoever he wrote, what he invented, yea all his devises, practises, and thoughts were of the subversion of England: Well, these Banners and Ensigns which he hoped to have displayed in England to our great reproach, were to his deep dishonour hanged to the joy of all true English hearts, about the Battlements and cross of Paul's, and on London bridge: . . .' A.B. Grosart, ed., *The Works of Robert Greene* (1881–3), V Prose, 158–9.

22. Elliot-Drake, I, 104–5.
23. PRO SP12/214/17-19; M. Lewis, *Armada Guns* (1961), 136–7, 143–4, 227, 232–5. It is odd for Alvarez to have exaggerated. His other facts were right, and he knew they could be checked.
24. PRO SP12/215/67.i.
    The list of guns, in descending order of weight (lbs), is as follows:

    bronze

demi-cannon	5230	fowler	803
ditto, 6" bore	—	great base	788
ditto, ditto	—	falconet	784
basilico	4840	great base	759
culverin	4736	great base	708
culverin	4728	great base	684
culverin	4589	base	390
culverin	3237	base	388
cannon pedro	3032	base	385
cannon pedro	3021	base	382
cannon pedro	2934	base	212
cannon pedro	2894	fowler	186
cannon pedro	2639		
cannon pedro	2566		

    iron

demi-culverin	2300	minion	1100

    These weights assume that the English simply copied the Spanish weights marked on the guns, though they sometimes translate the tens and units into quarters (of 25 lbs) and pounds.

25. PRO SP12/213/42 (Laughton, I, 326–7).
26. PRO SP12/215/67; 218/4 (Laughton, II, 190–92, 289–91). Was the gun on the *Samaritan* the one taken off in Torbay, or was that an extra missing one?
27. Lewis, *Armada Guns*, 227–32. The one gun whose weight we know from Spanish sources, the culverin moved from the *Duquesa Santa Ana*, weighed 3193 *libras* (AGS CMC 2a 1210). No gun of this weight appears in the English inventory, so it may be that this large gun was one of the 'borrowed' ones. The *Roebuck* was a 300 ton ship, the *Samaritan* 250 and the Chance 60.
28. PRO SP12/215/68 (Laughton, II, 188–90).
29. PRO SP12/218/4 (Laughton, II, 289–91). Lewis considered that the gun at Portland must have been a heavy one, to be of use on a castle (*Armada Guns*, 228–9).
30. *APCE*, xvi, 346–7, 27 November.
31. *Ibid.*, 380, 19 December.
32. *APCE*, xvii, 89.
33. R.B. Wernham, *After the Armada* (1984), 20–1, 110.
34. Hakluyt, 321, 323, 326, 339. As the largest guns in the inventory of the *Rosario* are three demi-cannon, a basilico and three culverins, it seems almost certain that these two demi-cannon and two culverins are Drake and Norris's choice from the *Rosario* guns.
35. *APCE*, xvii, 395, 18 June. In fact, although the ship had passed into the charge of William Hawkins of Plymouth on 2 May 1589, it had not left

Dartmouth. But there was obviously confusion as to whether or not she had been moved to Plymouth.

36. PRO E351/2226.
37. H.L. Blackmore, *The Armouries of the Tower of London, I Ordnance* (HMSO, 1976), 269, demi-culverin, 3021, portpeece hall, 775; BM Add Mss 34,808, (1599), culverin, 3021 (*Rosario* cannon-pedro 3021, falconet, 775). Portpeece hall and falconet could be the same guns, but the lower the weight, the more likelihood of two or more guns weighing the same.
38. A.C. Carpenter, *The Cannon of Dartmouth Castle, Devon* (Plymouth, 1984), and pers. comm. The English inventory lists a demi-culverin of 2300 lbs (probable bore 4½ ins), and a minion of 1100 lbs (probable bore 3¼ ins).
39. PRO SP12/214/17, 18, 19.
40. *CSP Spanish*, no. 466, p. 477.
41. PRO SP12/213/59.i (Laughton, I, 303).
42. PRO SP12/213/42 (Laughton, I, 326-7), 5 August.
43. PRO SP12/214/17, 18, 19.
44. AGS GA 221/151.
45. *APCE*, xvi, 188.
46. PRO SP12/213/59 (Laughton, I, 338), 8 August.
47. PRO SP12/218/4 (Laughton, II, 291).
48. PRO SP12/213/47; SP12/215/49, 49.i, 49.ii, 49.iii (Laughton, I, 334; II, 151-8). 'It is credibly thought that there were in her 200 Venetian barrels of powder of some 120 [lbs] weight apiece, and yet but 141 were sent to the Lord Admiral.'
49. AGS GA 221/151.
50. AGS CS 2a 274.
51. AGS GA 221/151.
52. PRO SP12/214/17, Alonso de la Serna, Alonso Vazquez, Pedro Martín Cabrito.
53. PRO SP12/215/67; 217/10 (Laughton, II, 186-8, 263-4), 16 October.
54. *APCE*, xvi, 250, 258.
55. R.G. Marsden, *Select Pleas in the Court of Admiralty*, (Selden Society, vol. XI, 1897), II, 180. This lawsuit, like many others, arose from disputes over Drake's will. Lake was in the end reprieved.
56. Pine, 13-14.
57. C.J. Ffoulkes, *Inventory and Survey of the Armouries of the Tower of London* (1916), 29; H. L. Blackmore, *The Armouries of the Tower of London, I Ordnance* (HMSO, 1976), 11.
58. BL Royal 17 A xxxi. These were carried by Spanish officers as a symbol of their rank.
59. Ffoulkes, 30. Unfortunately he gives no source for his statement that weapons were sold to provide money for rewards. 'Various weapons and implements of war which have been employed against the English by different enemies, now deposited in the Tower of London' include 'A Spanish lance for bleeding the English', 'The Spanish General's spontoon', 'A Spanish battle-axe with a pistol at the end', 'A Spanish Morning Star to keep off people from boarding ships', 'A Spanish shield with a pistol fixt in it', 'A Spanish instrument of torture called the Cravatt', 'A Spanish bilbo to lock the English by the legs', and 'The Pope's banner by him christened Invincible'. A 'Spanish General's shield' mentioned in Ffoulkes's text but not in

illustration, is now thought to be from Brunswick, but the 'Pope's Banner', still in the collection of the Tower of London, is a Spanish shield dating from the sixteenth century, and may be one of the few genuine Armada relics. I have to thank Mr Angus Konstam of the Royal Armouries for this information.

60. PRO SP12/214/17, 18, 19.
61. AGS CMC 2a 1012. The *Rosario* loaded 402 barrels at San Lúcar in July 1587. From February to May 1588 at least 54 were added. The *Trinidad Valencera*, with fewer men on board, set off with at least 350 barrels of wine, and 21 were added at Corunna (AGS CS 2a 280/1463, 1465).
62. PRO SP12/215/68 (Laughton, II, 189).
63. PRO SP12/215/67 (Laughton, II, 187).
64. PRO SP12/215/68 (Laughton, II, 189).
65. *APCE*, xvi, 293, 24 October.
66. PRO SP12/217/10 (Laughton, II, 263).
67. PRO SP12/217/21 (Laughton, II, 277–8).
68. PRO SP12/218/4 (Laughton, II, 291), 15 November.
69. *CSP Domestic, 1591–94*, 274. Gilbert and Cary disagreed over musters.
70. *APCE*, xvi, 329–30.
71. PRO SP12/218/14 (Laughton. II, 292–6).
72. *APCE*, xvi, 378–80, 19 December. The same day the Council wrote to the mayor of Plymouth 'to receive of the captain of the *Roebuck* all such things as are contained in the schedule enclosed'. As the schedule has not survived, we do not know whether this order concerned goods embezzled from the *Rosario*.
73. PRO SP12/213/89 (Laughton, II, 104–8), undated, but probably 21 August.
74. PRO SP12/214/63–4 (Laughton, II, 102).
75. PRO E133/47/4.
76. Elliot-Drake, I, 93.
77. H.P. Kraus, *Sir Francis Drake: A Pictorial Biography* (Amsterdam, 1970), 170.
78. PRO SP12/215/67.i (Laughton, II, 193–4), 7 September.
79. PRO SP12/217/22 (Laughton, II, 278–9), 24 October.
80. *CSP Spanish*, p. 492, no. 481, 27 November, 'The latter ship sank whilst they were bringing her from Dartmouth to Dover, and only two or three of the 60 sailors on board of her were saved . . .' *CSP Spanish*, p. 492, no. 483, 3 December, 'The ship . . . was being taken from one place to another to be overhauled and made seaworthy again, when she was lost with her guns and the Englishmen on board'—with a note in the king's hand 'It must be Don Pedro de Valdés' ship. Better so than that they should enjoy it.' In fact it was the *San Salvador*, PRO SP12/218/24 (Laughton, II, 296–8). 23 men were lost, including 6 Flemings and Frenchmen, part of her original crew.
81. Marco Antonio Messia (*CSP Spanish*, p. 494, no. 485) said that the ship was offered to Drake and Norris. They certainly asked for the use of the *Victory* because of her size. The *Rosario* was bigger, but she was not designed as a warship, and she needed repair.
82. *APCE*, xvii, 143–4. William Hawkins died on 17 October 1589 and was buried in Kent. Was he there because he had personally supervised the moving of the *Rosario* to Chatham? M.W.S. Hawkins, *Plymouth's Armada Heroes* (Plymouth, 1888).

83. The ship had been totally in Gilbert's control. Cary lived at Cockington, near Torquay, whereas Gilbert lived at Greenway, on the Dart estuary. So the ship was moored close to his estate (see below, p. 45).
84. *APCE*, xvii, 315–6.
85. PRO E351/2226.
86. BL Add Mss 9294.
87. PRO SP12/240/24, 28 September 1591.
88. M. Oppenheim, *The Administration of the Royal Navy, 1509–1600* (1894), 121.
89. PRO E351/2256.
90. PRO E351/2260.

CHAPTER THREE

The Fate of her Crew, and of the Men from the San Salvador *and the* San Pedro Mayor

> ... *what shall become of these people, our vowed enemies? The charge of keeping them is great, the peril greater, and the discontentment [of] our country greatest of all, that a nation so much disliking unto them should remain amongst them.*
>
> (Gilbert and Cary to the Council, August 1588)[1]

WHEN Don Pedro de Valdés surrendered to Sir Francis Drake, he was joined aboard the *Revenge* by about 40 of the officers and gentlemen from the *Rosario*. The rest of those aboard were taken with the ship to Torbay and, like the ship herself, entrusted to the care of Sir John Gilbert and George Cary, deputy-lieutenants of Devon, who noted that

> there is almost 400 soldiers and mariners, all which ... we have taken out of the ship and brought them under safe guard unto the shore, some 20 or 30 mariners only excepted, which we have left in the said ship to be the better help to bring the said ship into safe harbour, [there] being at this present, through the occasion of her Majesty's service, great want of mariners of our own country.[2]

The Privy Council ordered Gilbert to sort out the prisoners,

> that those of name and quality might be discerned and known from the rest and bestowed in safe prisons; the rest of baser sort to be distributed into such prisons as he should think fittest ... or else kept aboard the ships ... with some spare and reasonable diet out of their own provision that remained in the ship.[3]

Most of those of 'quality', however, had never come to Torbay, but had stayed on board the *Revenge*.

When Gilbert and Cary made the inventory of the *Rosario* they admitted having given one cask of wine to

> my Lord Edward Seymour, for cumbering his house with these Spanish prisoners until the ship was cleared, not knowing otherways where we should have bestowed them.[4]

Lord Edward Seymour lived at Berry Pomeroy, but he also owned Torre Abbey, and so was a neighbour of Cary, who lived at Cockington, near Torquay. There is an old barn in the grounds of Torre Abbey still called the Spanish Barn, and this is probably where nearly all the prisoners were housed while the ship was being repaired.

When the ship was moved to Dartmouth, the prisoners were moved too. Gilbert and Cary reported to the Council as follows:

> Touching the said prisoners, being in number 397, whereof we sent to my Lord Lieutenant [the Earl of Bath] five of the chiefest of them, whom his Lordship hath committed to the town prison of Exon; . . . we have put 226 in our Bridewell, amongst which all the mariners are placed, which are 61, besides younkers and boys. The rest, which are 166, for the ease of our country from the watching and guarding of them, and conveying of their provision of their victuals unto them — which was very burdensome unto our people in this time of harvest — we have therefore placed them aboard the Spanish ship, to live upon such victuals as do remain in the said ship; which is very little and bad, their fish unsavoury and their bread full of worms, and of so small quantity as will suffice them but a very small time.[5]

On the same day Cary wrote to Walsingham, asking

> for some directions touching these Spanish prisoners, whom we would have been very glad they had been made water spaniels when they were first taken. Their provision . . . is very little and nought. . . . The people's charity unto them (coming with so wicked an intent) is very cold; so that if there be not order forthwith taken by your Lordships, they must starve. They are many in number, and divers of them already very weak, and some dead.[6]

In response to this appeal, the Privy Council decreed that it was 'her Majesty's pleasure that the Spanish prisoners for their relief should be allowed to every each of them 4*d* per diem'. This would

> be rebursed them here again upon their account, which allowance her Majesty is pleased should continue until some order shall be taken for their ransom and dimission.[7]

On 16 October Cary wrote to the Council again, protesting that this flat rate payment was not fair.

> In this service Sir John Gilbert and I do not agree: for he, being unwilling to take any pains where no profit ariseth, would fain thrust the 226 prisoners which remain at Bridewell, 16 miles from my house, to my charge. And he would take upon him the charge of 160 of the said Spanish prisoners remaining a-shipboard hard by his house, and every day hardly labouring in his garden in the levelling of his grounds, so that he is too wise for me (as he thinketh) to have their daily labour and yet allowance from her Majesty of 4d per diem to each of them. I have no grounds to level nor work to set them unto, so far from my house; and therefore, under your Lordships' favours, the match he offereth me is not equal.

He went on to suggest that Gilbert should only get 2d per day for those in his care.[8] His complaint was fair. Cary lived at Cockington near Torquay, and after the ship was moved to Dartmouth and the prisoners to the county Bridewell near Exeter, it was difficult for him to carry out his responsibilities, and there was no way in which he could turn them to his advantage.[9] Gilbert, however, lived at Greenway, on the eastern side of the Dart estuary, about two miles above Dartmouth. The *Rosario* was moored almost at the edge of his estate, and he was getting hard work out of the prisoners he was responsible for. This was wise, as the 4d a day was a promise of repayment in the future, not an advance or even a regular reimbursement. This is shown in Cary's continuing correspondence with the Privy Council. On 24 October he wrote saying that the 211 prisoners 'remaining in our house of correction near the city of Exeter' were in some distress. He had personally allowed each of them 1½d per day, and some of them 2d,

> for otherwise they must have needs have perished through hunger, and possibly thereby have bred some infection, which might be dangerous to our country.

He asked for money at once, saying that it would be cheaper if supplies could be bought in advance,

> for I dare assure your Lordships that 2d per diem, with some other allowances for fire and other necessaries, will suffice for their maintenance.[10]

On the same day he wrote to Walsingham,

> And whereas their Lordships, by their former letter . . . did allow 4d per diem to each of them, I will assure your Honour that they may be

very well maintained for 2d per diem, so [provided] that their Lordships will appoint some money to be received beforehand to buy their provision.[11]

But Cary's hope that the prospect of the prisoners costing less than budgeted might encourage the Council to produce some cash came to nothing. It seems that they agreed to reduce the rate, but failed to produce any money, so that in the end Gilbert and Cary had to protest that the allowance was not enough. But still no money was forthcoming; 'In answer to divers letters sent by them to their Lordships', the Council replied at the end of November that,

> where their Lordships were advertised that 2 pence the day is too scant to maintain the Spaniards taken in that ship, it seemed reasonable . . . in respect of winter season that a greater proportion might be appointed them, to which end they might confer with such merchants in those parts as trade to Spain how some convenient sum of money might be gathered or borrowed, if otherwise it cannot be had, upon some reasonable consideration, which shall be repaid again of such money as shall be paid for their ransom.[12]

The Council had taken some note of Cary's complaints, however, for on 19 December they advised Sir John Gilbert that money from the sale of wine and other goods from the *Rosario* should

> be employed towards the answering of such charge as they have and shall be at for the diet and other provisions for the Spanish prisoners of that ship placed near Exeter . . . [but] their Lordships think not fit that any larger allowance should be made to the prisoners remaining in Don Pedro's ship under his [Gilbert's] custody than 2d per diem, with some small allowance of fire this winter, in respect he doth daily receive the benefit of their labour.[13]

When on 2 May 1589 the Privy Council ordered Gilbert to deliver the *Rosario* into the care of William Hawkins of Plymouth, they asked him to continue to be responsible for the prisoners, 'until their enlargement [release] may be obtained, to which end one was sent from the Prince of Parma.'[14]

* * *

On the same day as the *Rosario* was crippled, another ship of the Armada, the *San Salvador*, had been badly damaged by an explosion and fire. The cause of this explosion was never known. It was probably an accident, though there were various stories at the time that it had been deliberately caused by a German gunner who had been cuckolded by a Spanish officer, or, in another version, simply reprimanded by one.[15] Whatever the cause, the results of the explosion were disastrous. As Ubaldino tells us,

> Both of the after decks were blown up, killing over 200 men . . . many of the men jumped into the sea and were drowned, but the principal persons were saved in four pataches sent by the duke [of Medina Sidonia]. Paymaster Juan de Huerta, his staff papers, and some money in his charge were saved.

The ship was taken into the middle of the fleet for safety. But the next morning it was decided that she was beyond repair, and

> the duke ordered the people to be taken out of her and the ship sunk. The captain, however, was badly wounded, and the men in a hurry to abandon the ship, so that there was no one to sink her; besides which, she had many wounded and burnt men on board, who could not be rescued as the enemy was approaching.[16]
>
> Lord Thomas Howard and Sir John Hawkins . . . in a small skiff of the *Victory*'s, went aboard her, where they saw a very pitiful sight — the deck of the ship had fallen down, the steerage broken, the stern burnt out, and about 50 poor creatures burnt with powder in most miserable sort. The stink in the ship was so unsavoury, and the sight within board so ugly, that the Lord Thomas Howard and Sir John Hawkins shortly departed . . .

They reported back to Lord Admiral Howard, who ordered Captain Thomas Fleming, in his bark the *Golden Hind*, to

> conduct her to some port in England which he could best recover, which was performed, and the said ship brought to Weymouth the next day.[17]

On 19 August Burghley, the Lord Treasurer, wrote to George Trenchard, 'vice-admiral of these parts', and Francis Hawley, a justice of the peace, at Weymouth, asking them to keep the prisoners safe until further orders, and to see 'whether there be any man of quality or great account amongst them.'[18] On 3 September Trenchard and Hawley replied that,

> we find here no Spaniards of any account, but only one who calls himself Don Melchor de Pereda, and nine others of the common sort; two Frenchmen, four Almains [Germans or Flemings], and one Almain woman; and since their landing here, twelve more are dead. We humbly beseech your Lordships to give some speedy direction what shall be done with them, for that they are here diseased, naked and chargeable.[19]

So it seems that by this time there were only 17 survivors. Even so, Trenchard and Hawley, like Gilbert and Cary, complained to the Privy Council about the burden the prisoners placed on the local area. On 10 January 1589 the Council replied that

> forasmuch as they [Trenchard and Hawley] desired their Lordships' resolution for the suppressing of the insolence and misdemeanours of the Spaniards which remained in the town of Weymouth Melcombe Regis, and put the inhabitants at great charges, their Lordships thought meet and so required them, as well for the discharging of that town of so great a burden as also for the good ordering of the said Spaniards and keeping them in due obedience without giving offence to her Majesty's subjects, that presently upon the receipt hereof they commit them and every of them to the next prison, there to remain and to be relieved only with bread and water until they should receive further order from their Lordships to the contrary.[20]

When the ship herself was being towed round to Portsmouth, she sank in Studland Bay. On 25 November it was reported that 'there was lost 23 men, whereof six of them was Flemings and Frenchmen that came in the same ship out of Spain.'[21] These were almost certainly the two Frenchmen and four Almains listed above, and they may have been on the ship because it had been decreed that all non-Spanish prisoners were to be freed (see below, pp. 51–2).

* * *

The only Spanish Armada ship to be actually wrecked on the coast of England was the *San Pedro Mayor*, and in her case only after circumnavigating the British Isles. According to a statement taken from some of the survivors,

> After they had sailed round the islands of England, Scotland, and Ireland, they were pursued by continual tempests; they were in want of food, and the ship was unseaworthy, and on the 6th November, 88, was driven ashore and wrecked at a place called Hope, belonging to Sir William Courtenay . . .[22]

Some others, after their return to Spain, gave a more detailed account, in which they told of their adventures in Ireland. Separated from the rest of the fleet by a storm, they had landed on 28 September at a place called Ross. They found there the wreck of the Levantine ship *San Nicolas Prodaneli*. They were told that about 60 men had survived, but they only found evidence of nine, who were imprisoned in the nearby town they called 'Calivia' (possibly Killala, in Co. Mayo). They negotiated with the local authorities in Latin to obtain the fresh water they desperately needed. But when ten men set off for food they met 60 English soldiers, and were taken to the same prison as the survivors from the *San Nicolas*. Pedro de Samillan and two others were allowed back to the ship to negotiate a ransom, but the English soldiers, on orders from their superiors, refused to accept the money, and executed the three men they still held. The survivors bought food, and on the 21 October they left the port of Ross, but had to anchor offshore to wait for the right wind to get safely clear of the coast of Ireland. When the wind changed, their anchor could not be lifted, so they had to cut the cable. They had sailed to within 30 leagues of Spain when the wind changed again. The ship was in such a sorry state that they could not afford to wait, so they decided to run for the coast of Brittany. But they found themselves instead being carried past Plymouth. They had no anchor, and were finally wrecked in Hope Cove five miles west of Salcombe, South Devon on 7 November. English boats came out and helped them ashore.[23]

Sir William Courtenay, of Powderham on the Exe estuary, was the present head of the family which had fallen victim to Henry VIII. He owned most of the land between Hope Cove and Salcombe, including Ilton 'Castle', a fortified mansion in the parish of Marlborough, less than two miles from Salcombe. It was barely two years since Mendoza, at the time of the Throckmorton Plot, had told Philip of Spain of:

> Sir William Courtenay, a Catholic, who expects to be able in the turmoil [of an invasion] to recover the earldom of Devonshire which is his by right. He is a person of great weight and credit in the west and promises to ensure the possession of the port of Plymouth.[24]

He had been sheriff of Devon in 1579–80 and was now one of the county's deputy-lieutenants.

George Cary, who had heard of the wreck while he was in Plymouth trying to recover embezzled goods from the *Rosario*, rode over to take charge. He reported that

> the ship is a hulk, and called St Peter the Great, one of those 2 ships which were appointed for the hospital to the whole navy. She is in burden, as they say, 550 tons, but I think not so much. The ship is not to be recovered; she lieth on a rock, and full of water to her upper decks.[25]

When members of the Privy Council heard about the wreck, on 11 November, they sent down one of their clerks, Anthony

Ashley, to supervise the salvage. They were hoping to prevent widespread theft from the wreck, having learned from the problems encountered by the local authorities delegated to guard the contents of the *Rosario* and the *San Salvador*. Gilbert, Cary and Ashley were to sort out the prisoners, reported to be 200, and to separate any 'of quality and calling' who might, on Ashley's recommendation, be sent to London.

> And for the rest of the soldiers and common people it was thought convenient they should cause them, being Spaniards born, to be executed, destroyed and dealt withal by martial law, as most pernicious enemies to her Majesty and the Realm.[26]

Cary reported to the Council on 15 November that about 140 men had survived the voyage.

> There are no men of account in the ship . . . I have severed the captains and chiefest of them, to the number of ten persons, from the rest; eight of them I left to the charge of Sir William Courtenay, and two of them, the one being the pothecary, the other the sergeant, I took to myself; the others are put in safe keeping, and guarded both day and night; and [I] have appointed 1½d a day to every of them, to make provision for their sustenance, until your Lordships' pleasures were further known; which I humbly desire may be with some speed, for that the charge of these, and those of Bridewell, grow somewhat heavy unto me . . . I would humbly desire the gift of those two Spaniards which I have, not for any profit, but to make trial what skill is in them.[27]

On 22 November Ashley wrote to the Council from Courtenay's house at Ilton, saying that he had relayed their orders to 'the gentlemen',

> for the deferring [sic] of the execution of the Spaniards, and do herein enclose a schedule of the names of those of the best sort, with their offices, quality, and their offers for ransom, as also of all the rest of the meanest sort, and likewise such of other nations as came in the ship; with such other particularities touching the said persons as I thought necessary . . . It may please your Lordships to signify your pleasure touching such of the company that are not Spaniards, as of the rest, as soon as your Lordships shall think convenient, for avoiding the charge of their diet. Those Spaniards that offer ransom will also pay for the charge of their diet until their departure, . . . and for the loan of the money for their liberty and growing charges, they would send some one or two to collect and bring over the same. Ten or 12 of the best sort are placed in a town called Kingsbridge, where order is taken for the provision of their wants and account kept of their expenses; the rest, until your Lordships' further pleasure known, are remaining together in one house, whither they were first committed, where they are safe kept and provided of necessary food.[28]

This was the last time that execution was mentioned, and there is no explanation as to why the Council changed its mind.[29]

The list Ashley made of all the survivors is still extant. Laughton published the names of the men offering a ransom, but the document is here reproduced in full with a comparison with two Spanish lists of hospital personnel (see Appendix B). There are 158 names on Ashley's list. According to the Lisbon Muster, the *San Pedro* carried 213 soldiers and 28 seamen.[30] This seems a large number of soldiers, especially since there must have been 50 or so hospital staff on board. A list of troop distributions at Corunna gives more likely figures of 34 seamen and 110 soldiers, with 93 hospital staff in the whole fleet.[31] According to Cary, the survivors said that they had left Spain with 30 mariners, 100 soldiers and 50 hospital staff.[32] Ashley categorised the survivors as 34 mariners (including the captain), 111 soldiers, three gentlemen, nine hospital staff and one clergyman. But it was not as simple as that. Some of the men, in all categories, were patients, and not part of the original complement of the ship. There were ten men from the *San Salvador*, and presumably some from other ships, such as Diego Soliez, page to Don Alonso de Leyva. A further complication is that the English clerk categorised people incorrectly. Amongst the soldiers, for example, there were included a clerk, two attendants of the sick, and two cooks; and among the Portuguese soldiers, a servant and the pilot. But whatever the exact figures, a large number of the original complement of the *San Pedro* seems to have survived. Although the figures are far from exact, it is interesting to look at the different survival rates among these various groups. One would expect that sailors would survive best, followed by soldiers, and that those men unused to fighting or life at sea would be most likely to die through accident or disease. From the figures for the *San Pedro*, the survival rates, in round terms, are: sailors, 100 per cent; soldiers, 90–95 per cent; hospital staff, around 50 per cent; clergy, 20 per cent (one out of five). Similarly, on the Spanish flagship, the *San Martín*, only two of the Duke of Medina Sidonia's 60 servants survived the journey.[33]

The prisoners' request to send an envoy to Spain to arrange their ransoms was not agreed to. On 27 November, however, the Council ordered Ashley to

> set at liberty such Flemings and Frenchmen as were taken amongst the Spaniards in a ship . . . called the Hospital, who were to return to their countries by such means as they might.[34]

A similar order presumably applied to the prisoners from the *San Salvador* as well (there were no Flemings or Frenchmen mentioned among the crew of the *Rosario*). But the remaining prisoners from the *San Pedro* were giving cause for concern. On 18 December the Council wrote to Sir William Courtenay, Sir Thomas Dennys and George Cary.

> Whereas their Lordships were advertised by letters from the above named that the Spaniards which arrived at Hope in the hulk called St Peters were greatly diseased, by reason whereof the inhabitants of those parts were likely also to be infected with the contagiousness of such sickness, their Lordships thought it convenient to will and require them to take speedy order for the avoiding of further inconvenience and that the Spaniards should be conveyed to certain barns and outhouses, standing apart from other tenements and dwelling places, there to be lodged and kept in such sort that none may be permitted to have access unto them, but only such as shall be by you appointed to have charge over them.

It was, after all, a hospital ship, and also the conditions on board after over three months at sea must have been very bad, and conducive to the spread of infectious diseases. The Privy Council then conveyed its newest money-saving scheme:

> and for that they were driven into this realm by chance, and came not of any set purpose, it was therefore thought by her Majesty and their Lordships that the country should yield them relief . . .[35]

In two months the Council had changed from demanding the execution of these men 'as pernicious enemies to her Majesty and the Realm' to claiming that they were shipwrecked on their way home, and were therefore not prisoners of war (to be paid for by the Queen), but a purely local charitable responsibility. The Council did, however, continue to give orders about the prisoners, as they were concerned that these men should remain safely in custody until they could be ransomed and sent back to Spain.

On 19 December the Council wrote to Sir William Courtenay, Sir John Gilbert and George Cary that

> six prisoners of the Spaniards which came in the hulk [were] to be by him [*sic*] received and kept at his own charge and so to remain, without either sending them beyond the seas or otherwise disposing of them, till further order be taken.[36]

From this ambiguous instruction onwards it is difficult to work out which prisoners were held where and under whose charge. At first eight prisoners were given to Courtenay, and Cary kept

Plate 1. An engraving by John Pine, published in 1739, from one of the tapestries commissioned by Thomas Lord Howard, now lost. The Rosario is in the left foreground, detached from the Spanish fleet sailing away to the right. To her left is the Margaret and John and immediately behind her is the Revenge, Drake's ship. The last of the English fleet is sailing out of Plymouth, top left. (National Maritime Museum, by kind permission.)

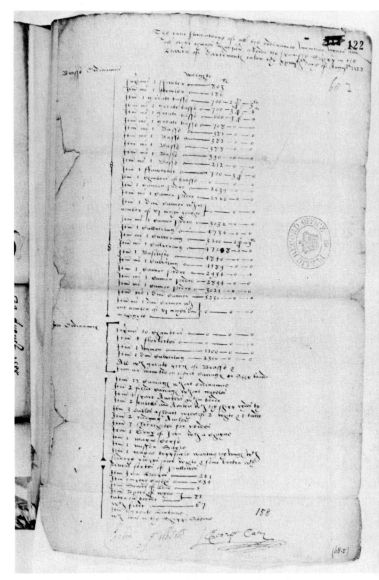

Plate 2. Inventory of the contents of the Rosario, 7 September 1588 (N.S.), signed by Gilbert and Cary. (P.R.O., SP 12/215/68i.)

Plate 3. John Pine's engraving (1739) of two of the Adams charts of the Armada, depicting on the lower border 'Sir Francis Drake distributing among his officers and sailors the money, etc., that was found in a great galleon brought to Dartmouth. Others are driving the prisoners before them.' (National Maritime Museum, by kind permission.)

Plate 9. Portrait of Richard Drake of Esher (1535–1603) in 1577, artist unknown. (National Maritime Museum, by kind permission.)

two. Then it was agreed that 13 of the 18 men of 'quality' could offer a ransom. Ten or 12 of them were imprisoned in Kingsbridge. In June 1590 there were 15 Spanish prisoners in the care of Courtenay, and they thought they were the only ones left.[37] In 1592 Gonzales del Castillo said that he was one of 12 imprisoned by Courtenay.[38] If these two groups were distinct, then one could represent the ten or 12 in Kingsbridge, and the other Courtenay's original eight, plus the six mentioned above. This seems to have been the case. According to Pedro Robledo (a surgeon, who did not appear on Ashley's list), the army captain, his ensign, both sergeants, the captain of the ship, Pedro de Samillon and seven others were held in a house (? Ilton Castle) in Marlborough, half a league from where they were wrecked. Robledo himself, with Lope Ruiz, was in Cary's charge.[39]

In January 1589, when Drake and Norris were preparing their expedition to Portugal, it was reported that 'all the Portuguese prisoners from the Armada had been released, on condition that they should embark in Dom António's fleet.'[40] The report named one prisoner in London, but presumably this order was applied in the West Country as well. If so, some or all of the 13 Portuguese men from the *San Pedro* may have been released.

* * *

During these months, while the costs and housing of the various prisoners were being discussed, negotiations were under way to ransom them. The Privy Council engaged Richard Tomson to negotiate on its behalf. He had served as a lieutenant on the *Margaret and John*, a 200 ton ship owned by Sir Walter Raleigh and paid for during the Armada campaign by the city of London, which was involved in both the capture of the *Rosario* and the looting of the *San Lorenzo* off Calais. In mid-September he reported to the Council on a meeting with Don Pedro de Valdés, in which he had told Valdés that the Council had agreed in principle to the ransoming of the ordinary prisoners, if Valdés could arrange for the money to be raised in the Low Countries. Don Pedro and his two fellow-prisoners, Alonso de Zayas and Vasco de Silva, had expressed their gratitude, saying that

> the said poor people were raised by them and were their neighbours, and came in this employment for the love and zeal that they bare unto them [Alonso de Zayas and Vasco de Silva had both recruited their companies of soldiers locally, especially for the Armada campaign[41]] . . . and they hoped . . . their Honours would consider

that they are very poor men serving the King for 4, 6, and 8 crowns a month, and that according to the same their Honours would appoint the ransom.

Tomson had replied that the ordinary soldiers would be freed for one month's pay, but the officers should expect to pay more, and any who were well-connected would be held back to be used to exchange for English prisoners in Spain, or else for a much higher ransom. Valdés had asked him to work first on the ransoming of the 'poor men, of whose misery they stand in great doubt if they should remain in prison until the cold of the winter approacheth.'[42]

Valdés wrote to Walsingham to thank him, and asking that someone should be sent to Parma with his letters of credit.[43] He wrote to Walsingham again on 24 September to say that Tomson had informed him that 390 of his men were to be freed for 10 ducats (£2 10s) each, and he had written to Parma to arrange payment and transport.[44] On 1 October, however, Tomson was instructed to ask Parma for 15 ducats per man, and to insist that the prisoners should return directly to Spain (so that they could not immediately serve against England in the Netherlands).[45] In November Tomson's proposals were presented to Parma, who expressed surprise at the amount being asked — one month's wages was the normal rate, and this is what he was prepared to offer, plus a small sum for their keep, 'paying promptly by exchange in London as her Majesty desires'. On 29 November Tomson was still waiting for a reply.[46] Apparently working in liaison with Tomson in the Netherlands was Juan Gonsalves de Salorzano, from the *San Lorenzo* (see below, pp. 71–2).[47]

After this nothing seems to have happened for several months. Those holding the prisoners were getting increasingly worried about all the money they had spent, and wondering whether they would ever be reimbursed. Valdés, too, was getting impatient.[48] Meanwhile, some of the men from the *San Pedro* seem to have acted independently. Pedro Robledo was let out on parole, because his skills as a doctor were in demand. Francisco de la Desma and Pedro de Samillan similarly seem to have had some degree of freedom. They established contacts with various merchants and sailors. Their first two escape plans failed. But while a large number of ships of different nationalities were being gathered in Plymouth for Drake and Norris's Portugal expedition the three men seized the opportunity to escape. They were back in Spain by February 1589.[49]

In June 1589 the Privy Council wrote to Sir Thomas Dennys and George Cary, saying that the money would be coming soon

> to which end [some]one was presently looked for here to be sent from the duke of Parma to take order for the redeeming of them. In the mean season, because their Lordships did understand by them that some of [the prisoners] did carry themselves very stubbornly, it was thought meet that they should chastise those disorderly persons and wilful amongst them, or [use] any other means that they should think fit to repress their insolencies and stubborn behaviour.[50]

On 4 June the Queen had granted a passport for an envoy from Parma to come and pay the ransoms,[51] and on 27 September she asked the States of Holland to ask the Admiral of Zealand to allow free passage from Dunkirk to Plymouth for the vessels to transport the prisoners.[52] At the end of July Tomson had informed Walsingham that the ransom money would be provided very shortly.[53] But there were more delays, and on Walsingham's instructions Tomson wrote to Parma that the Privy Council would 'dispose of the prisoners' unless the ransoms were immediately ordered. By 4 September Tomson heard that the ransom money had been paid to the commissary at Antwerp, but it would take a month or two for it to get to London.[54]

On 18 October 1589 Pedro Cubiaur acknowledged the passport, and said that he would leave Dunkirk for Dartmouth on the next tide with three flyboats.[55] On 22 November the Council wrote to the Earl of Bath, Lord Lieutenant of Devon, explaining that the Spaniards were all to leave from Dartmouth. They understood that, because of the plague, Dartmouth itself had not enough forces to guard the men and quell any possible disorder, and they asked the Earl

> to give order unto his deputy lieutenants that some of the [militia] bands of that count[r]y next adjoining to the said town may be placed there for their better assurance and safety, to continue and remain there until such time as the said Spaniards shall be embarked.[56]

The prisoners were mostly soldiers, and there was a chance that when gathered together they might attempt some action, although probably all they really wanted to do was get safely home at last.

On 24 November they were officially freed.[57] Philip II, in a letter dated 30 January 1590, rejoiced to hear of their release, and asked Parma now to work towards the ransoming of those who had been held back (mainly the prisoners in London).[58] In March the Venetian ambassador wrote to the Doge that

> 470 soldiers, who were prisoners in England, have been liberated; their ransom was 16 scudi apiece. The King paid a part of this sum . . . these men were placed on board two ships which reached Corunna at the middle of last month.[59]

The third ship arrived at Ferrol at about the same time.[60] If the Venetian figure of 470 is correct, does it account for all the prisoners in the West Country? The number of prisoners from the *Rosario* decreased from 397 on 7 September 1588 to 391 on 16 October, and 376 or less on 24 October.[61] So by the end of 1589 there were possibly between 350 and 370 survivors. Of the 17 from the San Salvador, six probably drowned in Studland Bay, and some may not have survived the winter. It is known that 158 men survived the wreck of the *San Pedro Mayor*. If the 13 Portuguese, ten Frenchmen, two Italians and ten Dutchmen were set free earlier, and we know a number of men were not released at this time, that leaves about 100, possibly less. Perhaps not all the non-Spaniards were released, but probably a number of men died during the winter. So the figure of 470 does seem to represent the total number of prisoners in the West Country, except for the few from the *San Pedro* who were not released.

According to a statement made in June 1590 by some of the remaining prisoners from the *San Pedro*, the agreed ransoms had been 100 crowns for captains, 50 crowns for ensigns, and 15 to 20 for other officers and soldiers.[62] It is not clear which prisoners this refers to, but it is almost certainly this main group. When they got back to Spain, these men claimed their arrears of pay, and it is from the Spanish archives that a few names can be attached to the prisoners from the *Rosario*. Antonio Griego, an *armero* (armourer or gunsmith), died in England. Ysidro from Genoa, a *lombardero* (gunner) who had served on the *Rosario* since 23 June 1587, was ransomed for 171 florins (£17). He returned to Spain in February 1590 on one of Pedro de Cubiaur's flyboats, and at once began to serve again as a *lombardero* on the galleon *San Medel*.[63]

But what happened to the men from the *San Pedro* who were not released? In June 1590 Antonio Rodriguez de Lucerna, one of a group of 15 still held by Sir William Courtenay was sent to France (with a certificate of good conduct from his sergeant, Bartolome Cano) to negotiate with the Duke of Mercoeur for their ransom. Courtenay was asking 20,000 crowns, which was quite unreasonable, and the Duke would only offer the same rate as had been paid for the main group, from 100 crowns for captains down to 15 for the lowest ranks.[64] And in March 1592 Gonzalo Gonzalez del Castillo, in France to negotiate on behalf of himself and 11 others, wrote an account of his sufferings at the hands of Courtenay.

> The 24 of November of the year 1589, the Spanish prisoners there were released by the Queen's order, excepting 12 which the Queen gave to Sir William Courtenay, who eftsoons straitly imprisoned us, requiring from us 5,000 ducats for our ransom; which sum was not paid, for that there were none save only poor men.

On 11 August 1590 Courtenay asked them for 12,000 ducats. Not knowing what to do, they wrote to the Queen, but their letter was intercepted by Courtenay, who

> thrust us into a strong prison, giving us for our diet but bread, broth and water. We were in such straits that, seeing ourselves dying, we resolved to break out of prison and appeal to the justices for a remedy; but they answered that they were unable to relieve us, because he [Courtenay] was a powerful man, with whom they could not meddle.

So they went back to prison. On 7 February 1591 Courtenay sent William Blake to Brittany to negotiate with the Duke of Mercoeur for their ransoms; but he was asking 25,000 ducats, and no agreement was reached 'so that the prisoners remain there to this day [9 March 1592]'.[65]

In September 1591 Philip II had written to Don Juan de Aguila, commander of the Spanish forces in Brittany, that he had heard that there were still some prisoners in England, who had written to Aguila about their release.

> We are seeking a man in the Armada hospital, who they say will be a convenient messenger to send thither to arrange for their liberation, but if you can devise any better or speedier means, you will adopt it.[66]

Gonzales del Castillo was sent to France as an envoy, leaving Exeter on 24 December 1591, but being forced back into Dartmouth by bad weather: eventually he reached Plymouth on 5 February 1592, and then Blavet, the Spanish headquarters in Brittany, where he wrote his account on 9 March.

In the same month Pedro Cubiaur wrote to Burghley that Sir William Courtenay was holding certain Spaniards prisoner and demanding an unreasonable ransom. Cubiaur, therefore, had arrested some English merchants and was holding them until the Spaniards were released.[67] And on 28 July the Privy Council wrote to Courtenay that the wife of a Captain Latham, captured in France, had asked if her husband might be exchanged for a Spaniard in his custody, Diego Dallox (presumably Captain Diego d'Aler), and they asked him

> to yield to some reasonable agreement between her and you for the diet of the Spaniard, whom as we are informed you have put to labour and to do you service, which if it be true, the composition ought to be more reasonable, so as she may by the exchange procure the delivery of her husband, being one that is very well recommended for his good service and deserves to be favoured for divers respects.[68]

Presumably this exchange was carried out, and the rest of the men in the custody of Sir William Courtenay were also eventually set free, though it is not clear exactly when or on what terms. It was perhaps typical of one who married as his second wife the widow of Sir Francis Drake and himself died a Catholic that he should not have scrupled to extract the maximum recompense from the Spaniards.

Meanwhile, on 9 February 1591, the Privy Council had written to George Cary of Cockington instructing him

> to continue in his safe custody one Lopee Ruisse, a subject of the King of Spain, who was taken in the hulk called the hospital and about two years past committed to his said custody as prisoner by Sir Francis Walsingham, until he shall receive order from hence to the contrary, not suffering him to have access or conference with any Spaniard, Portugale or other suspected person.[69]

And he was not the only stray prisoner. Since 1588 there had been other batches of prisoners, notably from Drake and Norris's Portugal expedition in 1589. In June 1596 the Privy Council decreed that any remaining Spanish prisoners should be treated more harshly, in retaliation for the treatment of English prisoners in Spain, and appointed Nicholas Osely to search out these remaining prisoners and put them in the Bridewell 'or some such prison of severe punishment', but

> there shall not any one of the said prisoners be dismissed and sent out of the realm without knowledge and satisfaction of the party whose lawful prisoner he is.[70]

At least one prisoner, however, seems to have remained in private hands, for in March 1597 the Privy Council ordered

George Cary of Cockington and his cousin Mr Cary of Clovelly to set free 'a certain Spaniard called Lopez Ruys de la Pegna . . . being but an apothecary and a mean man'. A son of Cary of Clovelly had been freed in Spain in exchange for Lopez Ruiz, at no charge,

> and also . . . the Count of Portalegre did cause him to be used very honourably and sent hither well apparelled as became a gentleman of his sort.

Cary of Cockington, however, had been holding on to Ruiz for years in the hope of a ransom, and refused to hand him over now without being paid for his maintenance,

> which manner of dealing we [the Privy Council] cannot but greatly mislike in gentlemen of your sort and reputation, being also dishonourable to the State.

The future Lord Deputy of Ireland was, then, no less inclined than other gentlemen to hold out for his rights, and more if it was to be had. The Council ordered Cary of Cockington to hand Ruiz over to their messenger, and Cary of Clovelly

> to send him in decent sort apparelled as your son was returned hither . . . wherein requiring you not to fail, we bid you heartly farewell.[71]

So, after nine years, Lope Ruiz de la Pegna was to go home. Was he the last of the Spanish Armada prisoners in the West Country?

Notes

1. PRO SP12/213/43 (Laughton, I, 328).
2. *Ibid.*
3. *APCE*, xvi, 199–200.
4. PRO SP12/215/68 (Laughton, II, 189).
5. PRO SP12/215/68 (Laughton, II, 188), 8 September. There were prisons in Exeter in the South Gate and under the Guildhall. Devon's only Bridewell was on the main road from the south a few hundred yards from Exe Bridge.
6. PRO SP12/215/67 (Laughton, II, 186), 8 September.
7. *APCE*, xvi, 269.
8. PRO SP12/217/10 (Laughton, II, 263–4).
9. Gilbert and Cary's accounts included 'for a boat of 12 tons to carry victuals to the Spanish prisoners to Bridewell, £2.' (PRO SP12/215/67.i [Laughton, II, 193]).
10. PRO SP12/217/21 (Laughton, II, 276–7).
11. PRO SP12/217/22 (Laughton, II, 278–9).
12. *APCE*, xvi, 346–7.
13. *APCE*, xvi, 378–9.
14. *APCE*, xvii, 143–4.
15. Ubaldino, 89; Calderon's account, *CSP Span.*, no. 439, p. 441.
16. Calderon's account, *CSP Span.*, no. 439, p. 441. According to the Jesuit de la Torre (BL Add Mss 20,915. ff. 42–8), over 200 died and 50 escaped.
17. Laughton, I, 9.
18. PRO SP12/214/55 (Laughton, II, 86–7).
19. PRO SP12/215/49 (Laughton, II, 152–3). They had another problem, too, as 'the carrack is so great as that she cannot be brought into this haven.'
20. *APCE*, xvi, 422–3.
21. PRO SP12/218/24 (Laughton, II, 296).
22. *CSP Span.*, no. 598, p. 583.
23. AGS GA 245/188. Pedro Robledo, Francisco de la Desma, Pedro de Samillon, 18 February 1589. I cannot locate Ross and 'Calivia' on contemporary maps. It is clear from other sources that they were in or near Mayo. Another possibility is that 'Calivia' is Galway, north west of which is a barony of Ross.
24. *CSP Span. 1580–86*, no. 469, p. 604.
25. PRO SP12/218/4 (Laughton, II, 290). The other hospital ship, the *Casa de Paz Grande*, never left Corunna (see Appendix B).
26. *APCE*, xvi, 328–9.
27. PRO SP12/218/4 (Laughton, II, 290–91).
28. PRO SP12/218/14 (Laughton, II, 292–4).
29. There was one report that Dr Lopez claimed to have been the means of 'saving from the gallows over 300 Spaniards from Don Pedro's ship, who had been sentenced to be hanged' (*CSP Span.*, no. 582, p. 574). This makes no sense in relation to the *Rosario*, but could possibly refer to the smaller number of men from the *San Pedro*. But it may well just be an idle boast with no basis in fact.
30. Herrera Oria, 399. The Lisbon Muster is a bit ambiguous, giving figures of 90 and 123 soldiers, but a total of 133!

31. Duro, II, 194–200. It is possible that troops were moved off to make room for extra hospital staff from the *Casa de Paz Grande* (see Appendix B).
32. PRO SP12/218/4 (Laughton, II, 290).
33. AGS Estado 455.
34. *APCE*, xvi, 347.
35. *APCE*, xvi, 373–4.
36. *APCE*, xvi, 380.
37. *CSP Span.*, no. 598, p. 583, 15 June 1590.
38. *CSP Span.*, no. 609, pp. 592–3.
39. AGS GA 245/188. Marlborough lies midway between Salcombe and Hope Cove.
40. *CSP Span.*, no. 501, p. 505.
41. AGS CS 2a 278/448.
42. PRO SP12/216/9 (Laughton, II, 215–6).
43. PRO SP12/216/10 (Laughton, II, 217).
44. PRO SP12/216/25.
45. *CSP For. 1588*, 214.
46. *CSP For. 1588*, 320–21.
47. *CSP For. 1588*, 321; *CSP For. 1589–90*, 355; PRO SP77/5/24.
48. *CSP Ven.*, no. 813, 14 February 1589, 'Pedro de Valdés . . . has now implored the king for the love of justice to condemn the Duke of Medina Sidonia to pay his ransom, and the ransom of all his ship's company, because the Duke failed to come to his rescue as he might quite easily have done. The king has endorsed the petition with his own hand.' This may be only a rumour, but a rumour reflecting Don Pedro's impatience.
49. AGS GA 245/188.
50. *APCE*, xvii, 278.
51. PRO SP12/224/67.
52. *CSP For. 1589–90*, 200.
53. *CSP For. 1589*, 408.
54. *CSP For. 1589–90*, 355.
55. *CSP For. 1589–90*, 357. Pedro Cubiaur had himself been a prisoner in England, released in September 1589 and sent back to Spain from Plymouth.
56. *APCE*, xviii, 219.
57. *CSP Span.*, no. 609, p. 593, Gonzalo Gonzales del Castillo.
58. *CSP For. 1589–90*, 357.
59. *CSP Ven.*, no. 916, p. 482, 1 March.
60. *CSP For. 1589–90*, 357.
61. PRO SP12/217/10, 217/21 (Laughton, II, 264, 276).
62. *CSP Span.*, no. 598, p. 584.
63. AGS CS 2a 275.
64. *CSP Span.*, nos. 597–8, pp. 583–4.
65. *CSP Span.*, no. 609, pp. 592–5.
66. *CSP Span.*, no 607, p. 587.
67. *CSP For. 1591–92*, 421.
68. *APCE*, xxiii, 32–3; *CSP For. 1592– 93*, 225 (PRO SP78/28/172, 174); *CSP Span.*, 601–4.

69. *APCE*, xx, 238.
70. *APCE*, xxv, 469.
71. *APCE*, xxv, 547–8. In May 1593, despairing of his return, and needing money for herself and her sons, Ruiz's wife, Maria Ortega de Medina, from Merida, had petitioned for his back pay. Ruiz, because of his absence, had not officially accounted for the medicines in his charge. His wife, supported by some of her husband's colleagues, was asking the authorities to accept, through her, Ruiz's statement that everything had been lost when the ship was wrecked. (AGS CS 2a 275).

CHAPTER FOUR

The Prisoners in London

Our pleasant country,
* so beautiful and so fair,*
They do intend, by deadly war,
* to make both poor and bare.*
Our towns and cities,
* to rack and sack likewise,*
To kill and murder man and wife
* as malice doth arise;*
And to deflour
* our virgins in our sight;*
And in the cradle cruelly
* the tender babe to smite,*
GOD's Holy Truth,
* they mean for to cast down,*
And to deprive our noble Queen
* both of her life and crown.*[1]

'THEN VALDÉZ with 40 or 50 noblemen and gentlemen pertaining unto him, came on board Sir Francis Drake's ship.'[2] All these men seem to have spent at least one night aboard the *Revenge*, but most of them were soon thereafter taken ashore by Thomas Cely, captain of the *Elizabeth Drake*, and Tristram Gorges, a neighbour of Drake's in Devon, who was presumably on board the *Revenge*. Drake's account book shows that escorting these prisoners ashore cost £112.[3] It is not clear where or when they came ashore, but on 7 August the Privy Council wrote to the bailiffs of a place called Kingston:

> whereas Captain Cely hath the charge to bring hither 40 Spaniards and 2 Englishmen, rebels and traitors to their country, which will be at Kingston this night, because the said Captain is appointed to bring the said English traitors hither to the Court, they are charged to cause the Spaniards to be kept there in some inn with good watch.[4]

And two days later they wrote to the Lord Mayor of London that

> whereas one Cely had brought up from Portsmouth xl and odd Spaniards, that his Lordship would see them in the night season conveyed to Bridewell, there to be entertained with such diet as English prisoners have in Spain, and to have a care that none be suffered to have access unto them, nor to suffer many of them to be together, whereby the house may be broken or any escape.[5]

Kingston is a common place-name in England, but the town referred to is probably the Kingston two miles inland from Portsmouth, on the road to London.[6] The Bridewell in London was just outside the city walls, where the river Fleet ran into the Thames.[7]

Unlike the case of the prisoners in the West Country, the names of a number of these 40 men are known.[8] They were:

Ship's company — Vincente Alvarez, the captain
Juan de Viono (or Viana), the master

Soldiers (officers) — Joseph Pelegrin, sergeant in the company of Alonso de Zayas
Marcos de Aybar, sergeant
Luis de Ribera, ancient bearer (*alferez*), from the port of Santa María
Alonso Vazquez, sergeant in the company of Pedro de Leon
Juan Gaietan, sergeant in the company of Pedro de Leon
Crístobal de Leon, ancient bearer
Juan Bermudez, ensign
Alonso de la Serna, *entretenido* (unattached officer), from Zafra

(others) — 2 brothers of Juan Bermudez
Diego de Campos
Mateo de Fries
Pedro Martín Cabrito, from Eijha
Diego de Carmona
Juan Beceril
Santiago

Others — Góngoro, doctor of physic
Gregorio de Sotomayor, Portuguese, royal *alguacil* (constable)
Don Sancho Pardo

On 11 August the Privy Council wrote to the Lord Mayor again, to say that as the Bridewell had no funds to keep the Spanish prisoners for any length of time, he should

> inform himself what merchants or others have any servants or friends in prison, either in Spain or in the Low Countries, who would be contented to bear the charge of the finding of the Spaniards here, upon hope to exchange and redeem the other.

The list sent back to the Council included 12 named and 19 un-named prisoners in Spain, and four named and three un-named in the Low Countries.[9] The Council also asked the Lord Mayor to

> depute Mr Alderman Barnes, Mr Alderman Ratcliff, and such others as he shall know to be of skill in the Spanish tongue, to take a note of the said Spaniards' names and qualities, and thereupon to examine apart the most principal and apparent men among them upon the interrogatories enclosed and to draw from them the truth of their knowledge . . .[10]

These interrogations took place the next day.[11] Only 14 interrogations survive on record. It is not clear why there are two sets of answers for Gregorio de Sotomayor, why Juan Gaietan's answers were recorded in Italian, or why these two men were not asked the same questions as the rest. Laughton published the list of questions, the answers given by Vincente Alvarez, the captain of the ship, and one set of answers by Gregorio de Sotomayor. Alvarez's answers are the fullest and most detailed; indeed often the others did not answer certain questions, or 'affirmeth as the former examinate'. Although the other interrogations are less full, piecing together details and comments from them gives a clearer picture of what these men knew and felt. There are many frustrating gaps in the information provided, because the inquisitors wanted political information, which most of these men were not interested in or likely to possess. There is only one account of the capture of the ship (which was irrelevant to the questioners), and that is from Juan Gaietan, because for some reason he was not asked the standard questions. These were:

1. *'When the fleet came from Lisbon?'*
    The answers to this are of little interest, except that they varied from 27 to 30 May, and five men could not remember the date at all.

2. *'Whether, at their coming on the seas, there was any proclamation or denunciation publicly made of hostilities with England. What was the contents of the same; and, if it were done by writing, where is the same?'*

'Proclamation was made aboard the ship with the sound of 3 or 4 drums' (Diego de Campos). Five of the men missed the proclamation because they were ashore. As soldiers, their concern was not political but practical; what they remembered was what was said about the division of potential spoils, although they varied in what they thought was said.

> . . . all those ships which they took of the Queen's should be for the King, and for the rest of the ships they should be divided amongst the soldiers and he that first boarded them and set up the King's banner should have a greater reward. (Diego de Campos)
> Whatsoever ship they should meet withall . . . and that should be taken . . . all such gold, silver, plate, pearls, and jewels . . . should be for the king and the rest whatsoever for the soldiers. (Alonso de la Serna)

3. *'Whether the intention of the fleet was to invade and conquer England or no; and who should have had the principal charge of that enterprise?'*

Most of the men agreed with Alvarez: they were only definitely told that they were to rendezvous with Parma, but it was generally assumed that their final destination was England, and that Medina Sidonia was to come under Parma's orders. Alonso de la Serna, however, who had been ashore and missed the proclamation, said that

> the report went while they were in Lisbon that they should go to Alaracha in Africa, but being at sea it was given out that they should come to join with the Duke of Parma.

4. *'Where they should have landed; and whether their meaning were to take the City of London; and what they meant to have done if they had taken it?'*

Alvarez said that they were to land somewhere within the river of London (the Thames estuary), and to sack any town they came to. Neither he nor any of the others named a specific place of landing. Some knew nothing about it. Góngoro said that Don Alonso (de Leyva) had tried to persuade the council of war to attack Plymouth, and 'after some debating of the matter it was agreed that if they could pass the haven with 20 ships abreast they would follow that advice', but the arrival of the English fleet stopped them. Don Sancho Pardo repeated a rumour that they would not be able to get into the river of London 'for that their ships were too great'. Obviously they had no idea of the size of the Thames estuary. Gregorio de Sotomayor said that he had heard at Lisbon and Corunna

> that there was a plot laid to set fire in divers parts of the city of London and to sack the same when it should be in an uproar and so to follow on to the court where the Queen should be and make what means they could to kill her.

Again, the soldiers' concern was with loot not politics;

> the two fleets having joined together their determination was to come for England and as he hath heard to the river of London, for that the report went it is the richest city in all the world but what should have been done having taken it he knoweth not. (Pedro Martín Cabrito)

5. *'What they meant to do with the noblemen, gentlemen, and other subjects of quality, as well of our religion as of the other?'*

Many were discreetly silent on this point. Juan de Viono summarised the general view that

> the intent was to conquer the land and set up the mass but to take away the lives and livings of none but such as should resist.

Gongoro added that

> the soldiers gave out in general speeches that they should all depart very rich from England and that they bare a great hate against Sir Francis Drake.

6. *'What the Englishmen should have done that came with them; and whether they had not especial direction whom they should spare and whom they should kill; or where were they to receive it; and what it was?'*

Viono said that 'they gave it out that they came to recover their lands and livings.' (For more details see below, pp. 74–6.)

7. *'What they have heard or know of any help or succour that they should receive upon their landing in England?'*

Alvarez reckoned that between one third and one half of the population would support them. Most agreed with him or said nothing. Alonso Vazquez said that he hath heard that upon their landing they would have great help of English Catholics so that their strength would be such as that the war could not dure long.

8. *'What forces did they look for out of France to join with them?'*
Alvarez said the Duke of Guise and 30,000 men. Most of the men said or knew nothing. Alonso Vazquez said that the general report was 15,000 men.

9. *'Whether the King of Spain would have retained this realm for himself, or given it to any other; and who that is?'*
Alvarez and Vazquez said that it was not decided between the King and the Duke of Parma; three said the King; Góngoro said that Philip II intended to install the viceroy of Portugal as governor.

10. *'What principal noblemen of the Spanish or Italian nation be in this fleet?'*
Alvarez said that there were 52 great noblemen, and then named a few. Góngoro said that

> there were in this armada 65 men of great title and great blood which were heirs and second brothers to dukes, earls, and lords, of whom some stayed at the Groyne [Corunna] and would not go forward.

Pelegrin said 'there are a great number of gents of great title but who they are he cannot tell because he is a stranger of Catalonia.'

11. *'What Englishmen they know to be in this fleet?'*
Most knew only those in their own ship, though Mateo de Fries mentioned Sir William Browne on the *San Mateo*, and Alonso de la Serna named two on the *San Mateo* (Browne and Ralph Lyassale), one on the *Rata* (Sir Gerald Geraldine, son to Sir James Fitzmorris of Ireland), and five who had gone overland to Flanders (the Earl of Westmorland, Sir William Stavely, Sir William Semper, one who calls himself 'viscount of Earland' and Sir Charles Pagett).

12. *'What treasure was taken in the ship wherein they were taken?'*
(See above, pp. 23–6.)

13. *'What ordnance, armour, munition, and other furniture; victuals, armour etc., was therein?'*
(See above, pp. 8, 26–31.)

14. *'What was the number of the vessels; and where they missed any?'*

    Alvarez said that there were 152, and they lost four galleys and two pinnaces. Eight others agreed with the losses, but their total figure varied — three said 152, three said 151, one said 154, one said 130. Pedro Martín said there were 150, and they lost the galleys and one hulk. Góngoro said that there were 155, and 'he did hear say there were 4 galleys lost with a hulk that brought the horses [the *David*].'

15. *'Whether there be any other preparation to come hereafter for the defence of this fleet; and what number of men, ships and furniture there are?'*

    Most were vague about the possibility of a second fleet, and had nothing to add to Alvarez's statement that there were a number of large ships being prepared in Lisbon to bring supplies to the fleet. The fullest answer was that of Gregorio de Sotomayor, who said that they left in Lisbon to carry further supplies

    > 30 ships great and small, whereof there was two Levantiscas of the burden of 500 or 600 tons, the rest were hulks and caravels of 200, 300 and 400 tons and barks of 100 and 150 tons, and because they were not thoroughly appointed with ordnance there was sent to the ships from Lisbon ordnance of brass to furnish them.

The soberness of these questions and answers contrasts with the rumours which quickly circulated. The translator of the Lisbon Muster added an imaginary collection of whips, chains and instruments of torture.[12] This propaganda was picked up by the ballad writer Thomas Deloney;

> And not content, by fire and sword,
>   to take our right away;
> But to torment most cruelly,
>   our bodies, night and day.
> Although they meant, with murdering hands,
>   our guiltless blood to spill;
> Before our deaths, they did devise
>   to whip us, first, their fill.
> And for that purpose had prepared
>   of whips such wondrous store,
> So strangely made, that, sure, the like
>   was never seen before.

> For never was there horse, nor mule,
>   nor dog of currish kind,
> That ever had such whips devised
>   by any savage mind.¹³

The next verses went into bloodthirsty details. Reports of these stories were sent back to Spain. Marco Antonio Messia reported that

> It is publicly stated here that the Spanish prisoners confess they had orders, if they were victorious, to kill every Englishman over seven years old. They say they brought two kinds of whips (*scoriati*), one for men and the other for women. In order that you may not think it strange for me to write you this, I send you two printed legends that are current here, one respecting the capture of Don Pedro de Valdés's ship, and the other about the Queen's visit to the army. [Deloney wrote ballads on these two subjects as well as on the whips] . . . This is the reason the people are so enraged with the Spaniards. Their anger would certainly be justified if the above and other similar things were true.¹⁴

But all sensible men at the time knew that they were not true. Ubaldino said that such rumours were spread by preachers who

> in public sermons, stated that the Spaniards were carrying in their fleet a large number of women of every kind, and . . . that in the Spanish ships were many instruments of torture with which to afflict the English people. These things being easily believed, the whole of the lowest and most credulous part of the people were moved to a mortal and dangerous hatred against all foreigners living there. But later it was proved by examining the otherwise severe military printed orders of the Duke of Medina that this [the carrying of women] could not have been true . . . and having found out that one part was false, the other remained ineffective; . . .¹⁵

Indeed the prisoners themselves seem to have regarded such rumours as a joke. Messia went on to say that

> Six prisoners are kept at the house of an English merchant, and I see them sometimes. When I tell them some of the things I have written above, they laugh at them.¹⁶

Some later writers, however, in their desire to vilify Spain and to glorify Drake, the English nation, and the navy, took such rumours more seriously. E.F. Benson wrote in 1927 that the Rosario carried

> a large supply of whips made of cord and wire, with which (so Don Pedro stated in his subsequent examination before the Lords of the Privy Council) the Spaniards intended to flog to death the English heretics.¹⁷

As well as being interrogated, the prisoners were stripped of their fine clothes. A list of these clothes survives. One wonders what they were left with, and imagines how cold they must have been. The clothes taken from Alonso de la Serna consisted of:

> a coloured cloak, with a gold lace round about it; a pair of breeches of cloth of gold; a jerkin, embroidered with flowers, and laid over with a gold lace.

And from 'the ancient bearer Bermudo':

> a cloak mandillion; and breeches of rash, laid over all with gold lace; and a blue stitched taffety hat, with a silver band and a plume of feathers.[18]

The 40 men from the *Rosario* who went to London were joined by some of the prisoners taken when the English sacked the galleass *San Lorenzo* as she lay grounded under the walls of Calais castle. When the captain had been shot dead, most of the men leapt overboard to escape, and many were drowned. Richard Tomson described how,

> The captain . . . being slain, and the most part of their soldiers fled, some few soldiers remaining in her, seeing our English boats under her sides and more of ours coming rowing towards her . . . put up two handkerchiefs upon two rapiers, signifying that they desired truce.[19]

One report, perhaps not very reliable, said that all non-Spaniards on the *San Lorenzo* were released on the spot.[20] Certainly very few prisoners seem to have been taken. One source said that 35 were landed at Dover.[21] On 27 August the Privy Council asked William Wackelin (or Machelin) of Dover to

> send up hither an ensign which he took in the galleass, to be here on Monday; the same is promised to be restored to him again or sufficient satisfaction to his contentment.

On 2 September he was paid 40s for this service.[22] On 8 September the Council also paid one John Batchelor 'for bringing five Spaniards from Dover hither and carting them back again'.[23] Presumably they were brought to London for interrogation, and then sent back to their captors. But others from the *San Lorenzo* stayed in London, where the prisoners were sorted out, and some were taken into private houses.

Alderman Ratcliffe, writing to Walsingham on 6 September, said that he and Alderman Barnes had hoped that they might have

> obtained your Honour's warrant for the making choice of some 3 or 4 of the Spanish prisoners there [Bridewell], who might answer us for the charge of the rest. During which time of our attendance, the chiefest of the prisoners have been taken away by others.

He warned that if he were not helped, he would

> be compelled . . . to make a general collection through the city for the maintenance of those Spaniards; which will be very unwillingly assented unto by the common sort . . .[24]

A list made on 15 September showed how the various prisoners were disposed.[25] Feriez de Zalzacer and four others was placed with Sir Walter Raleigh. As Raleigh was the owner of the *Margaret and John*, which was involved in the sacking of the galleass, these men were presumably from that ship. *Alferez* Jironimo de Tixeda, also from the galleass *San Lorenzo*, was lodged with Sir Edward Hoby; Juan Gonsalvez de Solorzano 'the true captain of the galleass',[26] with Richard Tomson; and Góngoro, the doctor from the *Rosario*, with Doctor Lopez.

From other sources we know that Juan Bermudez and five others were lodged at the house of an un-named English merchant,[27] and that Diego de Campos was the prisoner of Doctor Hector.[28] Seventeen men from the *Rosario* remained in Bridewell, along with Rodriguez de Mendoza from the *San Lorenzo*. Mendoza wrote two letters to Walsingham thanking him for his kindness and asking him to take pity on him.[29] He also seems to have been involved with Horatio Palavicino in financial deals for ransoming the prisoners from Ireland.[30]

On 24 September Marco Antonio Messia wrote to Spain

> This letter will be accompanied by another written in Spanish by those who were taken from Don Pedro de Valdés' ship. I wish to serve one of these prisoners, as I know some of his relatives . . . Since the letter was written I have been negotiating for his ransom, and that of another ensign named Juan Bermudez, and two soldiers, his brothers; 500 crowns was the sum asked, and they offer 350, which they say they have means of obtaining, but nothing has yet been settled. The intermediary, however, hopes to arrange it for 400 crowns, which they will pay of they can do no better. . . . The other prisoners are in Bridewell, and it is said to be the intention to liberate

them on ransom, and apply the money to those who were wounded on the fleet; but they wish to ascertain whether those who undertake to pay ransoms have really the means of paying it.

Later in the letter he said

> I went today to see the Spanish prisoners in Bridewell. Two of them have become Protestants, one a Sardinian and the other an Andalusian, and they have been released, but I am told that those who refuse to listen to the preaching . . . are not allowed any share in the alms.

And on the question of ransoms 'very few of them have the means of paying a single penny, unless they are helped by their country'.[31]

Early in October Messia reported that in order help to sort out the prisoners in Ireland

> they have sent some men from here who take with them two of the men captured with Don Pedro de Valdés . . . who have both adopted this religion.

If their conversion had been a bid for freedom, they cannot have been very pleased at this move. He continued

> Last week there died one of the Spaniards in Bridewell, Alonso de la Serna, and there are many of them ill. They suffer much, especially as winter is coming on and they do not have enough clothes to cover their nakedness. My heart aches for them, but I have not the power to help them.

Another letter a few days later told the same story.[32]

In January 1589 Bernadino de Mendoza wrote to Philip II that

> All the Portuguese prisoners from the Armada had been released, on condition that they should embark in Don Antonio's fleet. I understand that a certain Juan de Sotomayor who was the royal alguacil in Don Pedro de Valdés's ship, is to go with the fleet, and a Seville pilot they took in one of the ships from the Indies, as well as all the Portuguese sailors . . .[33]

At the end of August 1589 those in Bridewell were joined by the prisoners sent over from Ireland.[34]

There is no clear reference to the ransoming of the prisoners in London. But it is possible that those who could offer no other ransom were included in the deal with Parma, and were sent home with those from the West Country. The fact that Gonzalez de Solorzano, from the *San Lorenzo*, was in the Netherlands in 1589, helping with negotiations, perhaps implies that some of the

London prisoners were included in this deal.[35] The rest must each have negotiated individually. Diego de Campos had been freed by Doctor Hector before April 1590, and he

> carried intelligences to the Duke [of Parma] . . . [who] gave him 14 crowns a month and gave him a letter to the King, to show him favour.[36]

Alonso Vazquez seems to have been released at the same time as Pedro de Valdés, and to have gone to Flanders, where he immediately returned to active service.[37]

★ ★ ★

Among the *aventureros* (gentlemen adventurers) and *entretenidos* (unattached officers) listed in the Lisbon Muster it is possible to identify about 20 English or Irish names.[38] There were also a number of Irish priests known from other sources, as for example Edward the Irishman and Jacob Brady, chaplains attached to the hospital.[39] Seven or eight of these English exiles were on board the *Rosario*. According to Vincente Alvarez

> two had come to court, one with Sir Francis Drake, and the rest, William Stukely, the pilot of the ship, Richard Brierly, and one more, passed forth of the ship before they were taken, promising to fetch them more aid.

Don Sancho Pardo said that

> he had conference with William Stukely, who told him that he had a brother that was a lord in this land and that upon the conquest of the land he should have his brother's lands given him by the king.

Juan Gaietan named Stukely, and also Henry Pickford, saying that they both fled.[40] So it seems that the four who left the ship were probably:

(a) William Stukely, listed in the Lisbon Muster, and recorded as having been paid by the King of Spain from November 1587 to September 1591.[41]

(b) Henry Pickford, who in 1591 was at Ferrol, receiving a pension of 10s from the King.[42]

(c) The pilot, almost certainly John Bonner, who was among the crew members claiming back pay when they returned to Spain, and who also appeared on the same list of pensioners as Henry Pickford, receiving 20s.[43] Cary had noted in a letter to Walsingham that 'the pilot of the ship is as perfect in our coasts as if he had been a native born.'⁴⁴ If Bonner escaped, did he have an English assistant, or had he trained a Spanish pilot well. Or was he in fact captured, but managed to conceal his nationality?

(*d*) The name Richard Brierly is not known from any other source, but a Richard Burley is listed in the Lisbon Muster. Burley, who came from Weymouth, and had lived in San Sebastian since 1580, was the best-known of the English rebels in Spain. He was later imprisoned in Spain accused of spying for England.⁴⁵

Another source said that William Stacey (the Guillermo Estachi in the Lisbon Muster), who was the brother-in-law of Alonso de la Serna, 'was saved from the ship in consequence of his having been sent, shortly before she was taken, on an errand from Don Pedro de Valdés to the Duke.'⁴⁶ Alvarez said that one man had gone with Drake. Juan de Viono and Juan Gaietan said that two stayed with Drake and Don Pedro. No more is heard about these men, or the one servant each brought by Stacey and Burley.

Two Englishmen, however, came ashore with the 40 men sent to London. They were sent up to London at once, ahead of the others.⁴⁷ One of these men was Tristram Winslade. On 18 September 1588 the Privy Council wrote to the lieutenant of the Tower of London, that

> whereas one Tristram Winslade remaineth in Newgate, heretofore taken in one of the Spanish ships, their Lordships' pleasure is that he be conveyed to the Tower . . . and to appoint a time of meeting for the examination of the said Winslade upon the rack, using torture to him at their pleasure.⁴⁸

He spent some time in the Tower, but on 6 March 1590 the Privy Council issued an order freeing him,

> for that he hath not only been often examined by Sir George Carey, Sir Walter Raleigh, Sir Richard Grenville, knights, Mr Attorney General and Justice Younge and others . . . but has been also upon the rack to draw from him his knowledge of the intended invasion, and being found by his examinations, and the reports of other men taken at the same time with him in the ship of Don Pedro, that he was brought hither aganst his will; and so taking bonds of him for his appearance at all times upon ten days warning to answer any [things] objected, this shall be [their] warrant to discharge him.⁴⁹

It is not clear who the other man was. One report mentioned that

> many English rebels went in the fleet, and amongst them, Richard Burley, and a brother of his, who, I understand is taken; if so, he can discover many things, and serve for a spy between England and Spain, for he has served the king in Flanders, and had 25 crowns a month, and there were many more such in the army.[50]

But in August 1590 the Privy Council referred to 'one Richard Stone, a principal party that came hither with the Spanish fleet prepared to invade the realm'; he was in the Marshalsea prison.[51]

The rack does not seem to have been very effective, for by 1600 Tristram Winslade was back serving in Stanley's regiment in the Low Countries, and was recorded as having served for a long time with Spanish forces in Flanders, Ireland and the Armada. According to a Spanish source he was 'a well-born gentleman, pensioned by order of the King'. He was said to be loyal, and to have 'endured much suffering'.[52] He had clearly misled his English captors.

Notes

1. Thomas Deloney, *A Joyful new Ballad* . . ., verse 9, in E. Arber, ed., *An English Garner* (1883), VII, 43.
2. Hakluyt, 376.
3. Elliot-Drake, I, 93.
4. *APCE*, xvi, 200.
5. *APCE*, xvi, 205.
6. S. Ogilby, *Britannia* (1675, facsimile edn Amsterdam, 1970), 30.
7. The building, originally a royal palace, was granted by Edward VI to the City of London in 1553. It was meant to be a place for rehabilitation of the unemployed rather than for penal incarceration, but it was also used for religious prisoners: e.g. O'Donoghue, *Bridewell Hospital*, I (1923), 184–5.
8. PRO SP12/214/16–19; SP12/215/78; SP12/216/5; *CSP Span.*, no. 437, pp. 437–38.
9. PRO SP12/216/6.
10. *APCE*, xvi, 210–11.
11. PRO SP12/214/16–19.
12. W.S. Maltby, *The Black Legend in England: the development of anti-Spanish sentiment 1558–1660* (Durham N C, 1971), 82.
13. Thomas Deloney, *A new Ballet of the strange and most cruel whips* . . . (10 Sept., 1588), verses 4 and 5, in E. Arber, ed., *An English Garner* (1883), VII, 52–6.
14. *CSP Span.*, no. 423, p. 421.
15. Ubaldino, 90.
16. *CSP Span.*, no. 423, pp. 421–2.
17. E.F. Benson, *Sir Francis Drake* (1927), 248.
18. PRO SP12/215/78 (Laughton, II, 209–10).
19. PRO SP12/213/67 (Laughton, I, 347–8).
20. *CSP Ven.*, no. 713, p. 376, the Venetian ambassador in France to the Doge, 15 August 1588.
21. *CSP Span.*, no. 400, p. 391. Advices from London, Antonio de Vega.
22. *APCE*, xvi, 239, 249.
23. *APCE*, xvi, 251.
24. PRO SP12/215/60 (Laughton, II, 170–1).
25. PRO SP12/216/5.
26. Ubaldino, 96.
27. *CSP Span.*, no. 437, pp. 437–8. Kingsbridge was a market town several miles inland.
28. PRO SP12/231/94, April 1590.
29. PRO SP12/215/74; SP12/218/5. In the second letter, on 15 November, he said that he was ill and miserable.
30. PRO SP12/223/32.
31. *CSP Span.*, no. 437, pp. 437–8.
32. *CSP Span.*, no. 440, p. 450; no. 444, pp. 454–5.
33. *CSP Span.*, no. 501, p. 505.
34. *APCE*, xviii, 60.
35. *CSP For. 1589–90*, 355; PRO SP77/5/24.

36. PRO SP12/231/94, April 1590.
37. AGS CS 2a 275.
38. Herrera Oria, 406–418; Duro, II, 66–75.

    Aventureros
    San Mateo, Rafael Sal (Ralph Lyassale) + 1 servant
    Don Guillermo Brun (Sir William Browne) + 2 servants.
    Santiago (Castile squadron) Dionisio (Irish)
    Entretenidos
    Don Mauricio Girardino (Sir Maurice Geraldine) + 2
    Admundo Estacio (Edmund Stacey) + 2
    Don Carlos Orconor (Sir Charles O'Connor) + 2
    Don Thomas Gualdino (Sir Thomas Geraldine) + 3
    Tristan Vinglade/Uniglade (Tristram Winslade)
    Ricardo Bereey/Burley (Richard Burley) + 1
    Roberto Lasec/Lario ?
    Juan Burner (John Bonner) + 1
    Don Pedro Murley (Sir Peter Marley) + 1
    Patricio Quimerfort (Patrick Kinford) + 1
    Diego Odor (James O'Dor)
    Roberto Rifort (Robert Riford)
    Ricardo Siton (Richard Seton)
    Guillermo Estachi (William Stacey) + 1
    Enrique Miguel (Henry Michael/Mitchell) + 1
    Roberto Daniel (Robert Daniel) + 1
    Tomas Bitus/Vitres, clerico irlandes, + 1

    No doubt there were other names which have been so successfully hispanicised that they have not been noticed. Alonso de la Serna named Sir Gerald Geraldine on board the *Rata*, and he does appear on an earlier list of *entretenidos*, though not on the Lisbon muster. (AGS CS 2a 278/4) Also on that earlier list was Sir Henry Ryan.

39. AGS CS 2a 281.
40. PRO SP12/214/16–19.
41. AGS CS 2a 284/447–8.
42. *CSP For. 1590–91*, 393, Boner, a pilot, 20s, Pickford 10s; *CSP Ireland*, 117, list of English pensioners at Lisbon, 'Mr Bonner, a pilot and gunner 30 ducats . . . Mr Pickford 12 ducats per month.'
43. AGS CS 2a 275, pilot and *entretenido*.
44. PRO SP12/215/67 (Laughton, II, 186).
45. *CSP For.*, passim; A.J. Loomie, SJ, *The Spanish Elizabethans: the English exiles at the court of Philip II* (New York, 1963), 66–8; *CSP Dom. Addenda 1580–1625*, 36–8, 255; *CSP Dom. 1591–4*, 101; PRO.SP12/231/94. He was in Flanders preparing for a spying trip to England.
46. *CSP Span.*, no.444, p.455.
47. *APCE*, xvi, 200.
48. *APCE*, xvi, p.273.
49. *APCE*, xviii, 387.
50. *CSP Dom. Addenda 1580–1625*, 255.
51. *APCE*, xix, 388.
52. Loomie, *The Spanish Elizabethans*, 263.

CHAPTER FIVE

Don Pedro de Valdés 1588–93

Don Pedro de Valdés, General of the Army of Andelusia, now Prisoner in England, grieving at his fortune, sitteth sad, and leaning his head on his hand, with a great sigh saith: 'Heu quanta de spe decidi'.[1]

ON 10 AUGUST 1588 Richard Drake was sent by the Queen on a fact-finding mission to the fleet, and brought this order to his (possibly very distant) cousin, Sir Francis:

> The Queen's Majesty would have Pedro de Valdés that was the captain of the galleon distressed, to be sent safe into England; and such other Spaniards as have been taken and are now kept on seaboard; for that she thinketh [it] very inconvenient to have any such kept upon any English ship, where either they may practise some mischief, or else come to understanding of the secrets of the services intended.[2]

Pedro de Valdés, therefore, had been on board the *Revenge* for ten days, and had presumably watched while the Spanish ships were chased up the Channel by the English fleet, culminating in the fireship attack on the Armada as it lay anchored off Calais. He must have seen the wreck and sacking of the galleass *San Lorenzo*, and then the battle of Gravelines, with the English fleet 'spending one whole day from morning till night in that violent kind of conflict, until such time as powder and bullets failed them.' The Armada had not been defeated, but it had been prevented from joining forces with Parma. During these ten days the English 'lost not any one ship or person of account', whereas

> the Spanish ships were so battered with English shot, that that very night and the day following, two or three of them sunk right down. . . .[3]

Drake immediately sent the prisoners ashore, with a letter to Walsingham, saying that

> I am commanded to send these prisoners ashore by my Lord Admiral, which had ere this been long done, but that I thought their being here might have done something which is not thought meet now. Let me beseech Your Honour that they may be presented unto her Majesty. . . . The one Don Pedro de Valdés is a man of great estimation with the King of Spain, and thought next in his army to the Duke of Sidonia. If they should be given from me unto any other, it would be some grief to my friends. If her Majesty will have them, God defend but I should think it happy.[4]

Drake's reason for keeping Valdés on board the *Revenge* for so long may never be known. Perhaps he was simply trying to make sure that he kept control of such a valuable prisoner. His letter was delivered by Tristram Gorges, who took the prisoners ashore at Rye and escorted them to London. For this service he was paid the large sum of £50 by Drake.[5] With Valdés were 'the captains of footmen, Don Alonso de Zayas of Laja, and Don Vasco de Mendoza y de Silva of Xerez de los Cavalleros, who had charge of the companies that were levied in those places.'[6] According to Bernadino de Mendoza, writing to Philip II on 20 August,

> As the London people were so alarmed, Don Pedro de Valdés and the rest of those who were captured . . . had been taken in carts to London, so that the people might see that some prisoners had been captured.[7]

On 14 August, two days after the prisoners in Bridewell had been interrogated, Don Pedro himself was questioned by the Privy Council. There are two sets of questions surviving, one with marginal notes of the answers, and one separate set of answers.[8] This interrogation seems to have been a formality, perhaps because it was known that most of the important information Valdés had to give had been revealed, wittingly or unwittingly, to Drake during the ten days Don Pedro was his guest on board the *Revenge*. The questions he was asked were in the same vein as those put to his subordinates. In many cases he denied any knowledge of Philip II's intentions, or refused to comment on them. To other questions he was very diplomatic. Asked how the King could justify an invasion of England, he said that 'it lieth not with him to answer if the King did well or ill, being a subject, and unable to judge the actions of his prince'.

He was asked for, and gave, very little of the factual detail which is of such interest to us now, but was irrelevant to or already known by his questioners. There are, however, a few points of interest. Asked 'which were their two places where they should have made their descent here in this realm . . .', he replied that 'it would be ordered by the Prince of Parma; except that if they met with foul weather, they intended to anchor at the Isle of Wight for to repair their damage'. He said that when they found out that the English fleet was in Plymouth 'the Duke called a council to consider of entering there and conquering the said fleet', but he (Valdés) had opposed such a move (see above, pp. 10, 66–7). When asked how much money there was on board, he said that there were about 20,000 ducats (see above, pp. 23–6), and 'vessels of silver worth another thousand'. To the question 'Which of the Englishmen in the army were privy to the secrets of the enterprise?' he said 'that none . . . are privy to the design'. The Englishmen on the fleet were there for their own reasons, and were useful to the Spaniards for their local knowledge and contacts, but none of them was important enough to be told much. Valdés also said that 'they have few pilots, whereof the most part are Spaniards and unexpert; and that there are few mariners'. His two fullest answers are about the decisions to proceed from Corunna, and not to enter Plymouth. In both these cases he was involved in the decision-making, and his advice influenced events. Were his answers fuller because he genuinely could not answer the other questions in equal detail, or did he become expansive in these instances because he could not resist demonstrating how important he was? Alonso de Zayas and Vasco de Mendoza were ordered to be interrogated at the same time, but their depositions have not survived.

As Don Pedro reported to King Philip, after he had been questioned, the Queen, at Drake's request, sent him

> four leagues off to a gentleman's house, called Richard Drake, that is his kinsman, where we receive the best usage and entertainment that may be.[9]

Richard Drake was an equerry to the Queen, and lived on his manor of Esher, in Surrey. One report said that 'the Queen was resolved to put him [Valdés] in the Tower, but Drake prevented it, as he was his prisoner.'[10] If this is true, the matter must have been resolved very quickly, for he was sent to Esher 'a good while before the return hither of Sir Francis Drake or Richard

Drake from the sea'.[11] Don Pedro wrote to Philip II from Esher on 31 August, giving his account of the loss of the *Rosario* (see above, pp. 10–12).[12] In September he was visited by Richard Tomson to discuss the ransoms of the prisoners in the West Country.[13]

Valdés and his two companions lived at Esher under house-arrest. When Richard Drake was away, a local JP had to be on the premises. On Walsingham's orders, 'Mr Lifield and his men lay in the said Mr Drake's house in his absence and locked the doors and kept the keys.'[14] They all went out hunting, and Don Pedro had at least one trip to London, for one Simon Wood testified in 1605 that

> as the late Queen's Majesty walked in St James Park and talking with the said Sir Francis and seeing the said Don Pedro in the Park, her said late Majesty did say unto the said Sir Francis . . . 'Drake, God give thee joy of this prisoner'. . . . Richard Drake had a weekly allowance from the said Sir Francis Drake of £4 for the said Don Pedro's diet which the servants of Mr Richard Drake came for weekly to the said Sir Francis or his officers at his house at Dowgate.[15]

Extra money was supplied on occasion, and 'Sir Francis Drake hath often times sent wine, oils, capers, and all other such provision as was sent for, for the said Don Pedro.'[16] According to Evan Owen, Drake also sent

> half a tun of claret wine . . . because my Lady Drake, wife to Sir Francis, did oftentimes lie a long while together at the said Richard Drake's house at those times that the said Don Pedro lay there.[17]

> And the said Richard Drake was likewise at great charge in giving entertainment to a great many that came to see him the said Don Pedro, as of noblemen, courtiers, citizens, and strangers that did sojourn within the land, and the country people dwelling thereabouts . . . Don Antonio, who was named the King of Portugal, his son, and divers others in his company did lie at his house, and Sir Horatio Palavicino and divers other strangers. And General Norris, Sir Francis Drake, with divers other commanders in the wars and many others of higher and lower degree, had great entertainment in that house by the occasion of the said Don Pedro his being there. And he willing to give them content and no offence to the Spaniards did often cause one to play upon a tabor and pipe in his hall and to set them to dancing and so brought in the Spaniards to see them dance whereby they might have some sight of the same Spaniards . . . and there was much beer drunk and much victuals spent in the said house at those times . . .[18]

Another of Don Pedro's occupations while at Esher was helping Mr Richard Percyvall, who was compiling the first Spanish–English dictionary. In his address to the reader Percyvall wrote

> after that I had collected it [the dictionary] . . . I ran it over twice with Don Pedro de Valdés, and Don Vasco de Sylva, to whom I had access, by the favour of my worshipful friend Mr Richard Drake . . .[19]

Life in house-arrest at Esher was then really quite comfortable, and it is clear that Valdés was several times threatened with removal to somewhere worse if he did not behave acording to the rules. There was a rumour in November 1588 that 'for having spoken ill of Don Antonio he is to be brought to London and put in chains.'[20] In February 1589 he wrote to Walsingham saying that Alonso de Zayas was very ill, and appealing not to be moved to a castle.[21] In August 1591 he was implicated in a conspiracy. A certain Moody was accused of plotting his escape, though it is not clear if there was any evidence of Valdés's involvement.[22] He was threatened with being moved to the Tower, and was perhaps transferred there briefly, but again it was Drake who we are told intervened on his behalf. According to Gonzalo del Castillo in March 1592,

> Don Pedro de Valdés lives, as hitherto, five miles from London. He was accused of an attempt to escape and imprisoned for it, but Francis Drake, to whom he always applies, settled the matter, and he now goes hunting and to other pastimes, the same as before.[23]

For the first few months of his captivity Valdés's concern was with the ransoming of the men on his ship. But once these negotiations were under way, he began to worry about his own position. In January 1589 he wrote to Philip II, appealing to him to pay his ransom.[24] But early in 1589 it was reported that 'Horatio Pallavicino has made great efforts to prevent any negotiation for the liberation of Don Pedro de Valdés, whilst the war lasts.'[25] Whether or not this was true, the Queen and her Council certainly seem to have decided that Valdés should be held on to until all the other Spanish prisoners had been ransomed, because he was their trump card. When the ransom of the bulk of the prisoners had been at last agreed, however, it was noted that negotiations for the release of Don Pedro and the most important of the prisoners from Ireland had encountered such difficulties that they had been abandoned.[26]

Alonso de Zayas also corresponded with Walsingham about his ransom. He was related to Gabriel de Zayas, one of Philip II's Secretaries of State, who was an old man. Don Alonso was concerned that if negotiations dragged on for too long his relation might die, and there would then be no-one who could pay his ransom. He also complained that he was short of clothes and miserable, and did not think that he could survive a second winter in England.[27]

As early as September 1589 it had been suggested that Valdés should be exchanged for Edward Winter, who was possibly a son of Elizabeth's Surveyor of the Navy.[28] This was an odd exchange, for Winter was not even a serving officer, but a private individual who had been unable to enter Dieppe harbour because of contrary winds, had been captured by a Spanish ship, and was being held prisoner in Le Havre. But the Queen seems to have regarded him as important, both in his own right and also with regard to his father's long service.[29] Drake also seems to have regarded Winter as a suitable exchange, for he sent a messenger to Esher who 'brought a letter in the belly of his doublet by which Sir Francis signified the taking of Mr Winter' and advised Don Pedro to write to Parma to get a guarantee that Winter would not be exchanged for anyone else.[30]

The Duke of Parma had at first demanded the exchange of all the Spanish prisoners in England and Holland for Winter and Odet de la Noue, seigneur de Teligny, son of the Huguenot leader Francois, who was in prison in Spain. But Teligny was exchanged for Don Alonso de Luzon and Don Rodrigo Lasso, the two most important Spanish prisoners from Ireland, and Parma then agreed to the exchange of Winter for Valdés.[31] Winter was therefore moved to Antwerp, despite promises made to him that he would not be moved to Spanish territory. Valdés wrote to the governor of the castle there, asking him to look after Winter, and not to punish him for trying to escape. Later he was moved to Brussels.[32] But negotiations proceeded very slowly. In August 1590 it was said that the King of Spain was very anxious to get Pedro de Valdés released, but the Queen would not let him go until peace was concluded. Winter had been offered, and then refused, permission to go to England on parole to negotiate the exchange.[33]

Discussions at Esher were conducted with the help of the scholar Richard Percyvall, who was often an interpreter between Mr Drake and Don Pedro and did often deal between Mr Drake and Mr Winter's men, and was the principal mediator (as he verily thinketh) of the resolution between them.[34]

After that Don Pedro had been at Richard Drake's house four years or thereabouts he fell to be very sick, and then the said Richard Drake grew fearful that the said Don Pedro would die and . . . that he would lose all the charges that he was at in keeping of him, which made him ever after the more earnest with the late Queen's Majesty and her Council to get order for his deliverance.[35]

And his pleading seems to have worked, for on 26 November 1592 the Privy Council wrote to Richard Drake to say that the exchange had been approved,

and if he shall by a day prefixed send Mr Winter to Calais, upon notice hereof Don Pedro shall also be brought thither at the same time, and exchanged in such sort on the water or otherwise as there shall be thought most meet . . .

The Council also wrote to Edward Winter that

her Majesty by the earnest solicitation of Mr Drake is contented that Don Pedro shall be forthwith put to liberty and exchanged for you, the charges of his ransom and otherwise to be defrayed by yourself as you know . . .[36]

It was February 1593, however, before all the necessary arrangements were made and Valdés was finally released.[37] He was given a farewell banquet by the Lord Mayor of London, and he took with him one John Standish, who was a convert to Catholicism. Standish wrote to his parents from Brussels that Don Pedro would not take him to Spain without their consent.[38] Alonso de Zayas and Vasco de Mendoza were ransomed for £900 each, and presumably left at the same time.[39]

They all set off from Billingsgate, Valdés cheerful because he did find that the master that was in the ship that broke his mast [was still] prisoner in England and gave God thanks that God had delivered him and left him (meaning the said master) who was the occasion of his taking, and imprisonment, in England a prisoner.[40]

He was escorted by Robert Drake, a nephew of Richard Drake, and Jonas Bodenham, a 'chief dealer for Sir Francis Drake', and indeed his right-hand man, in one of the Queen's ships.[41]

The ransom paid was £3,550. Winter paid £2,500 (£1,000 down, and the rest to be paid later), and Valdés himself £1,050, plus the maintenance for himself and three others, set at £400 per year (23 ducats per person per week).[42] On 13 March 1593 Valdés wrote a fulsome letter of thanks to Burghley from Brussels. In it, however, he complained about his host, claiming that Richard Drake was demanding too much money for his (Valdés's) keep, and asked Burghley to argue his case with the Queen and Council.[43] When Winter got back to England he complained about having to pay Valdés's ransom, and he too had a dispute with Richard Drake. On 2 May 1593 Sir Robert Cecil wrote to Winter, warning him that quarrels amongst those at Court might mean the loss of royal favour, and saying

> Mr Drake doth confess that you must pay £2,500, of which (his charge considered and venture of four years' time) we think him worthy. And for the sum [paid] by Don Pedro, we think you ought no way to meddle in it, as a matter not grievous to you what an enemy parts with to a gentleman that hath friended you and is your fellow in court.

Winter replied that

> after almost four years of barbarous imprisonment, after the racking me with infinite devices to pay £4,500 for my ransom and other charges, after the spending of the sweetest time of my youth in all melancholy (in all of which Mr Drake hath been the principal meddler)

if, after this, he had lost his temper, he should be forgiven. He had hoped for some sign of royal favour on his return. He promised to pay all that he owed Richard Drake, for

> it hath never been my meaning to withold one farthing, neither would I have the world esteem me so base as to take more reckoning of saving myself some few hundred pounds than of my reputation and true credit.[44]

Valdés spent over a year in Brussels, during which time he wrote letters and gathered information. On 19 March 1593, for example, he wrote to Philip II, with news of shipping, and a suggestion that he should secretly buy back a captured Spanish ship, presumably the *Madre de Deus*,

> ... the Indian ship they have taken is at Dartmouth, where they are trying to sell her. If your Majesty wishes to buy her, seeing the lack of ships there must be in Spain, it can be arranged through merchants without it being known ...[45]

In March he informed the King that he was going to inspect the coastal defences of Flanders.[46] And in a letter from Antwerp on 21 May he told Philip II that he received regular reports from England every ten days. He also asked the king to consider repaying his ransom, as had been done for the other prisoners such as Pimentel and Luzon.[47]

In the spring or early summer of 1594 Pedro de Valdés finally left Flanders for Spain.[48] In May 1595 he was paid his arrears of salary up to 31 July 1588. The rest of his arrears were paid to his heirs in 1624. Valdés's salary was 3,000 ducats per year. The total payment for his ransom, bribes, and the cost of his keep while in England came to 28,853 ducats.[49] Valdés had had to pay a higher ransom than any other prisoner, yet received far less in rewards when he got home. However, in 1602 he was appointed governor of Cuba, where he served until 1608. Then he retired to Gijon, where he died in 1614.

Notes

1. Robert Greene, *The Spanish Masquerado* (1589), in A.B. Grosart, ed., *The Works of Robert Greene* (1881–3), V Prose, 158–89.
2. PRO SP12/213/69 (Laughton, I, 356). The questions Richard Drake was sent to ask were basic ones such as the number of ships involved and the amount of powder and shot expended, and the losses on both sides, and also 'why the Spanish navy hath not been boarded by the Queen's ships . . .?' This was a difficult and expensive exercise. Drake had to be paid 'for his charges in going to Dover and from there to Sandwich where he did embark and understanding by such vessels as he did meet on the seas that her Majesty's navy was gone far northwards so as it was a great adventure to find the same . . .' (PRO E351/2225). If this was the case, it is not clear how Sir Francis Drake got the message about his prisoners so quickly, or why they were put ashore at Rye, and not further north.
3. Hakluyt, 386–8. The *María Juan* was the only ship sunk by the English in battle. The *San Felipe* and *San Mateo*, badly damaged, were wrecked on the banks of Flanders.
4. PRO SP12/213/73 (Laughton, I, 364).
5. Elliot-Drake, I, 93.
6. PRO SP12/215/36 (Laughton, II, 136). The third army captain, Pedro de Leon, had been sent to the *San Martín* with a message (presumably he was the *caballero* who accompanied Góngora), and then was sent on with another message to Parma. So he escaped both the capture of the *Rosario* and the rest of the fighting. He wrote to Valdés in November expressing his sorrow and offering to do anything he could to assist Valdés and the other prisoners. (*CSP For. 1588*, 305)
7. *CSP Span.*, no. 396, p. 386.
8. PRO SP12/214/20, 21, 22 (Laughton, II, 24–9); BL Lansdowne Mss. 96, ff. 148–9.
9. PRO SP12/215/36 (Laughton, II, 136).
10. *CSP Span.*, no. 470, p. 483, 5 November 1588, Marco Antonio Messia. The Spanish liked to hear stories about Don Pedro and the other prisoners being treated badly.
11. PRO E133/47/4, Evan Owen.
12. PRO SP12/215/36 (Laughton, II, 133–6).
13. PRO SP12/216/10.
14. PRO E133/47/5, Samuel Pomfrett, confirmed by Evan Owen.
15. PRO E133/47/3, Simon Wood.
16. *Ibid*, Simon Wood and his wife Margaret, servants at Dowgate.
17. PRO E133/47/4, Evan Owen.
18. PRO E133/47/5, Evan Owen.
19. Richard Percyvall, *Bibliotheca Hispanica* (1591).
20. *CSP Span.*, no. 474, p. 486, Marco Antonio Messia.
21. PRO SP94/3/38.
22. *CSP Dom. 1591–94*, 92, 99.
23. *CSP Span.*, no. 609, p. 594.
24. AGS.GA.224/256; *CSP For. 1589*, 69.
25. *CSP Span.*, no. 507, p. 513, 24 February, Marco Antonio Messia.
26. *CSP Ven.*, no. 916, pp. 482–3.

27. PRO SP94/3/43, 19 March; 94/3/91, 7 July; *CSP For. 1589*, 157, 345. In fact, Gabriel de Zayas did not die until 1595.
28. *CSP For. 1589–90*, 294.
29. *Ibid*, and *CSP For. 1592–93*, 346.
30. PRO E133/47/5, Richard Percyvall.
31. *CSP For. 1589–90*, 349–50.
32. *CSP For. 1589–90*, 294, 349; Valdés's letter to Mondragon, PRO SP12/239/91.
33. *CSP For. 1590–91*, 376–7.
34. PRO E133/47/5.
35. PRO E133/47/4, Evan Owen.
36. *APCE*, xxiii, 300.
37. AGS CS 2a 275; Archives Generales du Royaume, Brussels, Secrétairerie d'Etat et de Guerre 15/57; G. Ungerer, *A Spaniard in Elizabethan England: the correspondence of Antonio Perez's exile* (1974), 126.
38. *HMC Cecil (Salisbury)*, XIII, 477, 5 February 1593; *CSP Span.*, no. 612, p. 596.
39. PRO E133/47/3, Eliano Calvo; Elliot-Drake, I, 102–3, says that Don Alonso de Zayas and Don Vasco de Mendoza were freed earlier, but gives no reason for this statement.
40. PRO E133/47/4, Evan Owen. If this was true, it seems unlikely that the ship's master's imprisonment dated from 1588. He had probably been captured later, on the Portugal expedition or through privateering
41. PRO E133/47/5, William Meredith, Richard Percyvall, Evan Owen.
42. BL Lansdowne Mss. 76 (*CSP Span.*, no. 611, pp. 595–6); PRO E133/47/5, William Meredith.
43. *CSP Span.*, no. 611, pp. 595–6.
44. *HMC Cecil (Salisbury)*, IV, 314.
45. *CSP Span.*, no. 612, p. 597.
46. *CSP Span.*, no. 613, p. 598.
47. Ungerer, *A Spaniard in Elizabethan England*, 124–30.
48. Archives Generales du Royaume, Brussels, Secrétairerie d'Etat et de Guerre 15/57.
49. AGS CS 2a 275.

CHAPTER SIX

Retrospect

Long the proud Spaniards had vaunted to conquer us,
  Threatening our country with fire and sword;
  Often preparing their navy most sumptuous
  With as great plenty as Spain could afford.
    Dub a dub, dub a dub, thus strike their drums:
    Tantara, tantara, the Englishman comes.[1]

THE BUBBLE of Spanish invincibility had been pricked. The capture of the *Rosario*, and the presence of the Spanish prisoners in England, was visible proof of the failure of Philip II's plans. It was quickly forgotten that the Armada's defeat was due as much to the weather and to Philip's overambitious design as to any positive action on the part of the English. Without the captured ships and prisoners it would have been more difficult for the English to claim a victory.

The capture of the *Rosario*, on the second day of the action, gave an enormous lift to English spirits. As Ubaldino wrote in 1589,

> Now this chance of a ship alone having been taken in that way was considered such a good omen for the rest of the enterprise, that in London there were great signs of joy, as the beginning of what was to follow which had not seemed credible before . . .[2]

The English, instead of being depressed that such a great fleet had got into the Channel at all, now felt that defeat was not inevitable. The Spanish also recognised this change of mood. Don Juan de Cardona writing to Philip II from Santander in November 1588 emphasised the importance of the loss of the *Rosario* in boosting English morale. And equally it lowered morale among the Spanish forces. For if a flagship was not given any help when it was in trouble, then no other ship would be, and captains would therefore not be inclined to take any risks.[3] By this time, moreover, after all the delays and difficulties the Armada had experienced before reaching the English Channel, some of the commanders must have already had serious doubts about the viability of Philip II's Grand Design. Meanwhile, Sir Francis Drake and his associates gained benefits from a physical inspection of the captured ship, and from talking to her officers. There is no evidence that Drake himself boarded the Rosario, but presumbaly one or more of his officers did. Colin Martin has argued convincingly that something changed the English mood from caution to confidence. It must have been that they no longer thought the Armada invincible, and in particular that they had identified the shortcomings of its gunnery—poor shipboard gun-mountings and drills, a wide range of systems of weights and measures, different nationalities, and a clumsy and divisive system of command. All this they could have learnt from the *Rosario* and her crew.[4]

It has never been clear at what point Howard found out that the Armada was not intending to attack the coast of England directly, but was under orders to rendezvous with Parma (and only if that rendezvous failed was he authorised to try to take the Isle of Wight). But it seems likely that this information too came from Valdés. If so, it is probable that the English commanders were told at the council of war held off Dover on 3 August, and this new information is the best explanation of their change of mood and tactics after this meeting. Mattingly half saw this.

> They had had four days to watch the Spanish system in action, and Drake and Howard may have learned more about it from their talkative guest Don Pedro.[5]

But Howard's tactics could be even better explained if Don Pedro had also divulged that Medina Sidonia's orders were not to attack England but to get his fleet safely through the Channel to join forces with Parma. According to Ubaldino, Valdés gave information about the number and type of ships, their equipment, the loss of the four galleys early on, and that 'they had not imagined that they would have to meet at sea any force which they could not overcome'. Later on, he wrote, when the Spanish fleet had anchored off Calais,

> The Lord Admiral, having heard through some source of information that the Duke had ready a great number of barrels and water and 10,000 picked infantrymen . . . saw that to prevent a junction [with Parma] he must force Medina to leave his anchorage . . .[6]

Intelligence, from whatever source, certainly played an important part in decision making, and much of it may have come from Don Pedro, though that can never be proved.

At the time, no-one closely involved on either side blamed Valdés for the loss of the *Rosario*. When the surviving ships had limped home to Spain, the Duke of Medina Sidonia was unpopular with the public, though not with the King, and the real scapegoat was Diego Flores de Valdés.

> Don Diego Flores de Valdéz, one of the council of war on board the Armada, who persuaded the Commander-in-Chief to abandon Don Pedro de Valdéz . . . has been imprisoned in Burgos on the King's orders. He is to be tried along with others who have failed of their duty on that occasion . . .[7]

His cousin, Don Pedro, however, became, in Mattingly's words, 'both in England and in Spain, something of a minor popular hero'.[8] There were those who questioned his actions. The criticism in England was not personal, however, but portrayed him as a typical Spaniard, whose proud boasting turned to cowardice in the face of adversity. The name and story of Don Pedro de Valdés was well known among all levels of society, as is shown by the various references to him in literature and drama during the next twenty years. He was referred to directly, as in Robert Greene's *Spanish Masquerado*, and a play by Thomas Heywood, and also indirectly, as when Marlowe called one of Faustus's friends Valdés, or Shakespeare, in *Pericles*, referred to 'the great pirate Valdés'.

Although not popular in Spain, Don Pedro was recognised as very good at his job. He was impetuous, and ambitious, and a great schemer and gatherer of intelligence. The impression given by the various sources is that Don Pedro and Sir Francis Drake got on well together. They seem to have been similar in character. But according to one English witness who knew him well,

> Don Pedro did often times say, if he had known before his taking that Sir Francis Drake's promises unto him at his taking should have been no better performed on the part of the said Sir Francis that he would never have yielded himself or his ship unto the said Sir Francis, whatsoever danger might have befallen him.[9]

We do not know what promises Drake had made. But no-one could have foreseen such a long imprisonment for Don Pedro, and this is probably what he was mainly referring to. But that was nothing to do with Sir Francis Drake. As the same English witness put it,

> Don Pedro had not lain so long a prisoner if the said Sir Francis Drake had any power in himself to set down a ransom for the said Don Pedro or to set him at liberty.[10]

Valdés naturally resented his long imprisonment because of its cost, and because of the interruption to his career. But by surrendering he had almost certainly avoided a much worse fate. In a damaged ship he would have little chance of fame and glory from dashing action. And the survival rate among his fellow commanders was not good. Medina Sidonia lived through the homeward journey, and the subsequent public disgrace, and served his King for a further 24 years. But Don Hugo de Moncada died at Calais; Don Alonso de Leyva died in Ireland; Juan Martínez de Recalde and Miguel de Oquendo died soon after returning to Spain; only Martín de Bertendona, Juan Gómez de Medina and Diego Flores de Valdés survived, and Diego Flores was disgraced. It is not clear what the other prisoners felt about Valdés, but perhaps they too came to realise that they may have done better, despite eighteen months or more in prison, than many of their fellow soldiers and sailors. A large number of those who survived the long journey back to Spain died soon afterwards of malnutrition or disease.

The prisoners' interrogations give a glimpse of the views of the middle and lower ranks. The Armada, in the mind of Philip II, was a crusade, and his instructions made that clear. But no feeling of religious fervour comes across in what the officers had to say. In fact they seemed remarkably vague about what they were doing and where they were going. They were just doing a job of work, and obeying orders, and had little understanding of or interest in politics. As would be expected, some of the fullest and most interesting accounts came from the most widely-travelled and best-educated of the prisoners; Vincent Alvarez, the captain of the ship; Góngoro, a doctor; Gregorio de Sotomayor, the royal constable; and Alonso Vazquez, a soldier who later in his life wrote a history of the Spanish wars in the Low Countries.

An incidental result of studying the capture of the *Rosario* has been the realisation that the early accounts of the Armada, especially that by Ubaldino, were more accurate than is often assumed. These were often ignored or discredited by Victorian and later writers building the myth of Drake, and transferring backwards in time a conception of the British Navy based on its successes in the Napoleonic Wars. Even Naish, in his introduction to a recent new translation of the Commentary, says of Ubaldino,

> his anxiety to please possible patrons and show off as the scholar and historian with literary graces has probably robbed his Armada narrative of any real value as a tactical or strategic history of the campaign . . .

He admits, however, that it is important because

> Ubaldino writes an interesting narrative, irritating because of its limitations but which has some little historical value because Ubaldino has a message from Drake, if only he could put it across the centuries.

Specifically, he says

> Perhaps it is Drake's opinion which is given by Ubaldino, that the excellent gunnery practice of the English fleet decided the battle above all.

And he recognises that 'Ubaldino obviously talked to the captive Don Pedro'.[11]

Recent work, however, has changed the emphasis in Armada studies. Records of all kinds are now used to check contemporary literary sources. Historians have also begun to look again at the vast collection of original documents, instead of working from calendared and edited papers. And archaeologists have excavated the remains of several of the shipwrecks. Both these fields of research have led to more study of practical details, and from this wealth of practical detail can be built up a picture which challenges many previously accepted views. And, incidentally, it has validated some of the detailed factual evidence in the early accounts which had been ignored by historians interested only in an overall picture. Both Ubaldino's account and Hakluyt's translation of Van Meteren contain factual details and unbiased judgements which have been unrecognised for a long time. Ubaldino was less biased in favour of Drake than many later historians. He recognised, for example, the overwhelming reasons for the appointment of Howard as Lord Admiral rather than Drake,

> a man born and grown up among freebooters, who would have found it irksome to practise the self-restraint admired by the ancient Romans.[12]

One of Colin Martin's conclusions is that the decisive difference between the two fleets lay not in the quantity or quality of the large guns on board the ships, but in the practical details of how efficiently they could be fired and reloaded. The English guns were manned by sailors, the Spanish by soldiers not used to working on board ships, and speaking different languages, while the guns and their equipment were manufactured according to a number of different systems of weights and measures. Ubaldino pointed this out, claiming that Elizabeth refused foreign help because she

> was very wisely counselled not to mix in any way ships of other nations with ships of her own, because very often diversity of languages . . . causes trouble and damage . . .;

and later

> they were all of one nation and language . . . while the attacking fleet was manned by crews of different race with strange officers, and a variety of customs and languages, and ideas.[13]

Maltby in *The Black Legend in England* wrote

> the celebrated pamphlet of Petruccio Ubaldino is like a breath of fresh air . . . while its accuracy is anything but unimpeachable, it represents an effort at serious reporting.

But although he noted Ubaldino's comments on the disadvantages of such a mix of languages and customs, he condemned him for 'an idle tale that has been repeated, and apparently believed, for generations'. Ubaldino's story was that the explosion on board the *San Salvador* was caused because

> An army captain aboard . . . had insolently beaten a certain Flemish gunner in the ship, it is not known whether on account of words connected with his work or on account of the wife of the gunner who was with him, as is the custom of his country . . .[14]

In fact, in the original this story sounds much less far-fetched than in later re-tellings. And, although there were officially no women on board the Armada, one of the ships wrecked off the coast of Norway was known as the 'ship of the married men', and seems to have carried Flemish or German soldiers and their wives. Among the survivors of the *San Salvador* was 'an Almain [Flemish/German] woman'.[15] So it seems that it was the custom of certain soldiers to be accompanied by their wives, and that Ubaldino's story is not as unlikely as it at first appears.

As for Hakluyt, he freely acknowledged that the Spanish fleet kept very good order, and that while it kept that order very little damage could be done to it.

> The Spaniards in their sailing observed very diligent and good order, sailing three and four, and sometimes more ships in a rank, and following close up one after another, and the stronger and greater ships protecting the lesser . . . the Spaniards . . . had many great vantages of the English . . . for that they were so nearly conjoined, and kept together in so good array, that they could by no means be fought withal one to one.[16]

The English knew that they were up against a very powerful enemy. Though they had the advantage of fighting nearer to home, they entered the fray with no knowledge of their adversaries' plans. They were also desperately short of ammunition. The capture of the *Rosario*, as we have seen, boosted English morale both in the fleet and ashore, and correspondingly upset many in the Spanish fleet. In addition, the powder stocks from the *Rosario* were very important to the English as they struggled to force the Armada away from the coast of Flanders and its rendezvous with Parma. The prisoners, too, were useful for propaganda purposes, as visible proof of English success. And the greatest benefit of all may have been the information gained from Valdés himself during the ten days he spent on board the *Revenge*. If Don Pedro de Valdés had not surrendered to Sir Francis Drake on the morning of 1 August 1588, events might have turned out very differently.

Notes

1. Thomas Percy, *Reliques of Ancient English Poetry*, R.A. Wilmott, ed. (1857), 295, *the Winning of Cales [Cadiz]*, based on a ballad by Thomas Deloney written in or before 1596.
2. Ubaldino, 90.
3. Herrera-Oria, 352–3.
4. C.J.M. Martin, 'The equipment and fighting potential of the Spanish Armada' (unpublished PhD thesis, University of St Andrews, 1983), 399–401.
5. G. Mattingly, *The Defeat of the Spanish Armada* (paperback edn, 1970), 254–5.
6. Ubaldino, 90, 95.
7. *CSP Venetian*, no. 793, p. 420, 24 December 1588, the Venetian ambassador in Spain to the Doge.
8. Mattingly, 254–5.
9. PRO E133/47/4, Evan Owen.
10. PRO E133/47/5, Evan Owen.
11. D.W. Waters and G.P.B. Naish, *The Elizabethan Navy and the Armada of Spain* (National Maritime Museum, Maritime Monographs and Reports 17, 1975), 70–2.
12. Ubaldino, 87.
13. *Ibid.*, 83, 88; Martin, 399–401.
14. Ubaldino, 89; W.S. Maltby, *The Black Legend in England* (Durham, NC, 1971), 83–4.
15. PRO SP12/215/49 (Laughton, II, 153).
16. Hakluyt, 380, 386–7.

Appendix A

[PRO, SP12/215/67.i]

The true inventory of all the ordnance, munition, wines, and all other things whatsoever aboard the Spanish ship in the haven of Dartmouth, taken the 28 day of August [OS], 1588.

Ordnance of Brass

	lbs	qrs	lbs
Imprimis, one fowler	803	0	0
Item, more, one fowler	186	0	0
Item, a great base	700	2	3
Item, more, 1 great base	700	3	4
Item, more, 1 great base	600	3	0
Item, more, 1 great base	708	0	0
Item, more, a base	385	0	0
Item, more, 1 base	382	0	0
Item, more, 1 base	388	0	0
Item, more, 1 base	390	0	0
Item, more, 1 base	212	0	0
Item, a falconet	700	3	0
Item, 5 chambers of brass	0	0	0
Item, a cannon pedro	2,639	0	0
Item, more, a cannon pedro	2,566	0	0
Item, a demi-cannon, without number, of 6 inches height	0	0	0
Item, more, 1 cannon pedro	3,032	0	0
Item, 1 culverin	4,736	0	0
Item, more, a culverin	3,200	1	9
Item, more, 1 culverin	4,728	0	0
Item, 1 basilico	4,840	0	0
Item, more, 1 culverin	4,589	0	0
Item, 1 cannon pedro	2,934	0	0
Item, more, 1 cannon pedro	2,894	0	0
Item, more, 1 cannon pedro	3,021	0	0
Item, more, 1 demi-cannon	5,230	0	0
Item, more, 1 demi-cannon, without number, of 6 inches in height	0	0	0

Ordnance of Iron

	lbs	qrs	lbs
Imprimis, 10 chambers	0	0	0
Item, 4 fore-locks	0	0	0
Item, 1 minion	1,100	0	0
Item, 1 demi-culverin	2,300	0	0

All which great pieces of brass and iron are mounted on their carriages a-shipboard.

Item, 12 carriages without ordnance.
Item, 2 field carriages without wheels.
Item, 4 spare anchors within board.
Item, 2 cables and anchors which the ship rides by.
Item, 3 cables on shore, whereof 2 white and a tarred.
Item, 2 kedging anchors.
Item, 7 shear hooks for yards.
Item, a graper [grapnel] of iron with a chain.
Item, a main-course.
Item, 1 mizen-sail.
Item, 1 main-topsail wanting the wings, with sundry ropes, some whole, some broken, with divers sorts of pullowes [pulleys].

Item, iron hoops	261
Item, empty casks	234
Item, sows of lead	5
Item, butts of wine taken overboard	85
which filled	67

Item, a great lantern which was in the stern of the ship.

Appendix B

[PRO SP12/218/14.ii. original spelling]

The names, offices, and quallitie, or place of all those persons that came in the hulk called St Peter the great which was driven into a bay called Hope, adioyning unto the groundes of Sir William Courtney and within two myles of Salcomb.

The monethlie paie of officers and of privat soldiours.		offers for ransome.
ducats		ducats
40	Diego de Allier, captain of 100 soldiers embarqued in the hulk, hath served in the Low Countryes in the tyme of Don Juan, as, ancient, in the tercio of Don Ferdinando de Toledo.	—
15	Diego de Salvateria, ensigne to the said captain.	20
12	Francisco de Silva, captain of the shippe.	—
25	Rodriguo de Calderon, comptroller of the hospitall, brother to Coque Calderon, Auditor-general of the armie.	80
8	Alsonso de Munnez gent, sergeant of the companie.	20
18	Pedro de Samillon, overseer of the hospitall.	60
—	Gonzalo and Luis de Castillo, brothers, gentlemen adventurers, of Granada.	150
30	Lopes Ruiz, of Medida in Stremadera, the chiefe pothecarie of the armie.	—
—	Gregorio de Taguada, had the chiefe charge of the sick.	30
10	Francisco de Medina, the wardrobe keep.	30
6	Diego Martinez, keeper of the victuall and diet of the sick; is brother to the phisician of Juan Martin de Recaldes.	30
10	Juan Martinez of Melgar, clarke of the hospitall.	20
—	Diego Soliez, gent, page to Don Alonso de Leyva; thinkes his master will redeeme him.	—
—	Francisco de la Dezima, distributor of the victuall and diet of the sick.	—
6	Pedro de las Gueuas stuard of the hospitall.	20
7	Pedro Hernandes, corporall of the companie.	15
6	Martin Ximenes, assistant to the pothecarie.	15

Theis following being ordinarie privat soldiors their paie 4 ducats the moneth.

	Bartholomeo Cano, an ould soldier.	20
	Alvaro de Castro, one of the clarkes of the auditor of the armie, Calderons kinsman.	20

x	Andreas de Strada, one of them that was in the burnt shippe.	20
	Francisco Ximenes.	12
	Alonso Cortesio de Marcia.	30
	Hernando Diez.	30
	Anthonio de Rodrigues.	15
	Juan de Savales of Tordesillas.	15
	Pedro Hernandez de Casorla.	20
	Anthonio Hernandez de Outrera.	15
	Silvestre Ximenes of Marchena.	15
	Pedro de Florez, out of the burnt shippe.	12
	Christoval de Xanches.	20
	Francisco Diego de Alpande.	15
	Anthonio Juannes, servant to the ancient.	12
	Symon Diez de Arazena.	12
	Diego de Ruis.	12
	Gaspar de Mondragon, out of the burnt shippe.	16
	Jheronimo de Varaguan.	20
	Juan Hidalgo.	12
	Diego Stiago de Cassalia.	16
	Balthazar Nietto de Merida.	12
	Christoval Martin.	12
	Pedro Martin of Galerosa.	12
	Martin Xanches de Galerosa.	12
	Juan d'Ortelio.	12
	Anthonio Rodrigues.	12

Spaniardes that can give no ransome, being soldiours

Thomas Gomez ⎱ theis attend
Ginez   ⎰ the sick
Juan Rodrigues
Francisco Hernandes
Anthonio de Bruones
  out of the burnt shippe
Francisco Garcia
Juan de Candelas
Juan Gonzales, the barber
Bartholomeo Domingues
Alonso Garcia
Juan Ximenes
Alonso de Burcia
Francisco de Ximenes
Francisco de Ruis
Martin de Perez
Juan Alson
Jheronimo de Molma
Alonso Domingues
Domingo de Meque
Mathias de Candelas

Pedro Martin
Francisco de Ferez
Diego Hernandez
Juan de Castilla
Bartholomeo de la Yerua
Domingo Fernandes ⎱ cosineros
Diego Xanches   ⎰ [cooks]
Bartholomeo de Sales
Blas Garcia
Andreas Ximenes
Pedro Garcia
Ferdinando Ximenes
Francisco Barco, the
  pothecary's man
Juan Calderon, the
  pothecary's son
Domingo Martin
Juan Alonso
Diego del Corro
Pedro Hernandez

Alonso Dias
Bernardino
Luis d'Arsona
Anthonio Preto
Pedro Ruis
Pedro Garcia
Juan Ruis
Anthonio Ruis
Andreas Granado
Bernardino Gateras
Christoval de Golasia
Gonzalo del Rio
Alonso Perez
Gonzalo Hernandez

Mariners

Bartholomeo
Martin de Sugero

Mariners of Galizia

Gregorio Bago
Ferdinando Nivero
Gregorio Nunnez
Domingo de Oya
Juan Gago
Juan Barera
Pedro Dorado
Gregorio Solina
Juan Hernadez

Frenche mariners

Vincent Peot of Morbeau
Luis Callo, of Bluet
Juan de Pole of Brest
Francois Haray of Bluet
Jean Luis de Penmarque
Jean Gendi of Morbeau
Law. Mandurdeau of Poitou
Jaque Boret of Olone
Jean de Harsang interpretor and stuard for the Spaniardes
Piere de Cap Blanc, of Bayonne

Italien mariners

Pedro de Xanches
Juan Serano
Pedro Camiles
Juan Conde
Gregorio Martin
Pedro Sulasar
Bartolomeo de Tolo
Bartolomeo Lopez
Juan de Castra
Juan de Cabrera } boys
Matheo Garcia
Salvador Pano
Damean Rodrigues
Jheronimo
Martin Delgado

Portugale soldiors

Gonzal, yaves, the pilotte
Luis Rodrigues
Domingo

Juan Fernandez, a boy
Cosme Dias, servant to Pedro Samillon
Anthonio de Sa
Martin de Fernandez
Francisco
Gaspar Caravallo
Juan Gonzales
Sebastian Alfonso
Martin Fernandez
George, a boy

Dutch mariners

Mighel Remes, a gonner[?] neere Hambrough
Jacob Herdiz of Amsterdam
Foulker Remes
Jacob
Hanse Hoffeman, brothers, of Hamboroughe
Adrian Mighelson of Westfalia
Jacob Williamson of Amsterdam
Henric Sneper
Cornelis Hanson, a boy
Cornelis Clas

Jusepe, of Genoa
Paulo Estefono de Aragosa, a shipp boye

[signed] John Gilbert
        George Cary
          Chr. Harris
            A. Ashley

Of theis Spaniardes eight or nyne are sick;
three others dead since they landed whereof one was a negro.
Some drowned not herre sett downe;
tenne saved out of the burnt shipp brought into Wiymouth.
There are onlie xii or xiiii that are men of anie reckoning.

                                      [signed] A. Ashley

The following summarise two Spanish documents relating to the staff of the Armada hospital.

1. AGS CS.2a.281, drawn up in April 1588, consists of a list of hospital staff, in various categories, with their salaries:
    7 clergy, earning from 20 escudos per month (the chaplain), down to 5 (the sacristan).
    16 doctors and surgeons, earning from 50 escudos down to 15.
    6 assistants to the doctors and surgeons, earning 6 escudos.
    8 barbers, the chief earning 10 escudos, the rest 8.
    9 nurses (male), earning between 6 and 3 escudos
    25 officials, such as steward (25 escudos), overseer (18), secretary (10), dispenser (6), cooks (6), overseer of the servants (8), keeper of the wardrobe (12), the sexton (3), and all their assistants (between 6 and 3 escudos per month)
    a total of 67 names.

The *San Pedro* survivors who appear on this list are:

Juan Martínez, chaplain, 10 escudos
Lope Ruiz, doctor/surgeon, 25 escudos
? Alonso Garcia, surgeon's assistant, 6 escudos
Pedro de Samillon, overseer, 18 escudos
Francisco de Medina, wardrobe-keeper, 12 escudos
Pedro de las Guevas, steward, 8 escudos
Diego Martínez, assistant keeper of victual and diet of the sick, 6 escudos
Bartolomeo de la Yerua, assistant to above ?, 4 escudos
Francisco de la Dezima, distributor of the victual and diet of the sick, 6 escudos
brother Gines, nurse, 4 escudos
Juan Gonzales, nurse/barber, 4 escudos
Pedro Garcia, nurse, 4 escudos
Juan Rodrigues, nurse, 3 escudos
Alonso Perez, sexton, 3 escudos

2. AGS CS.2a.278/620-21, drawn up in May 1588, lists the hospital staff according to the ships on which they were embarked. There are 111 men listed, mostly by name. There are more clergy than in the other list, and more servants and assistants.

> 36 of them were scattered throughout the fleet in ones, twos and threes, including brother Navarro on the *Rosario*. Then there were
> 14 on the *San Marcos* (a Portuguese royal warship)
> 30 on the hulk *Casa de Paz Grande*
> 31 on the hulk *San Pedro Mayor*

The *Casa de Paz Grande* is recorded as having left Lisbon and arrived at Corunna, but not as leaving Corunna. Looking at the names of those assigned to the *Casa de Paz*, a number of them appear amongst the survivors from the wreck of the *San Pedro*. So it appears that, for whatever reason, the *Casa de Paz Grande* was abandoned at Corunna, and her medical staff transferred to other ship, probably mostly to the *San Pedro*. This might also explain the discrepancies between the number of troops listed on the *San Pedro* at Lisbon and Corunna. If more medical staff were added to the ship, perhaps soldiers were taken off to make room for them.

From the 30 men assigned to the *Casa de Paz Grande* we can identify 3 definite and 3 possible men on the English list:

Diego Martínez, keeper of the victual and diet of the sick
Francisco de Medina, the wardrobe-keeper
Juan Rodriguez, a nurse
? Domingo de Layba, nurse,
? Christoval de Xanches, ? dishwasher
? Francisco de Ferez

There was also a doctor Góngora, who may be the same as the one later taken prisoner from the *Rosario*.

From the 31 men assigned to the *San Pedro Mayor*:

Juan Martínez, chaplain
Alonso Garcia
Martin Ximenes, assistant to the pothecary
Juan Calderon, assistant
Pedro de Samillon, overseer
Pedro de las Guevas, steward
Bartolomeo de la Yerua, assistant to sexton
Francisco de la Dezima, distributor of food
Domingo Fernandez, assistant cook
Domingo Martín, nurse

The comparison of names between these lists shows that the English clerk has included the lower grades of the hospital staff amongst the ordinary soldiers in his classification of the prisoners.

It must be pointed out that there are 3 names which appear on the list of survivors but not in either Spanish list:

Gregorio de Taguada, chief nurse,
Thomas Gomez, nurse
Francisco Barco, assistant to the apothecary

Pedro de Robledo, who wrote an account of his experiences on board the *San Pedro Mayor* (AGS GA.245/188), does not appear on the English list. On the first Spanish list he was a surgeon earning 15 ducats per month. On the second list he was assigned to the *San Salvador*.

Index

Adams Charts, 31
Aguila, Don Juan de, 57
Alaracha, Morocco, 66
Alcega, Don Diego de, 6
Aler, Diego d', army captain, 58, 100
Alfonso, Sebastian, 102
Alonso, Juan, 101
Alpande, Francisco Diego de, 101
Alson, Juan, 101
Alvarez, Vincente, captain and part-owner of *Rosario*, 6, 25, 27, 29–30, 32, 64–9, 74–5, 93
America, Spanish, 3, 6–7
Andalusian squadron, 6–8, 10, 15, 19
Antonio, Dom, Portuguese pretender, 53, 73, 82–3
Antwerp, 55, 84, 87
Armada, Spanish, 29, 37, 53, 73, 76, 79, 90–1;
    captured weapons from, 31;
    in Channel, 4, 10, 16;
    as crusade, 93;
    early accounts of, 93-6;
    good order kept by, 96;
    invasion of England by, 9;
    planning and preparation of, 6, 8;
    shipwrecks from excavated, 94;
    steeped in bureaucracy, 22;
    women on board, 95
Army of Flanders, *see* Flanders
Arsona, Luis d', 102
artillery, *see* guns
Ashley, Anthony, clerk to the Privy Council, 33, 49–51, 53, 103
Attorney General, 75
aventureros, *see* gentlemen adventurers
Aybar, Marcos de, sergeant, 25, 64

Bago, Gregorio, mariner, of Galicia, 102
ballads, 1, 69–70
Barco, Francisco, pothecary's man, 101, 105
Barera, Juan, mariner, of Galicia, 102
Barnes, Mr, Alderman of City of London, 65, 72

Barrow, J., biographer of Drake, 1
Bartholomeo, mariner, 102
Batchelor, John, 71
Bath, Earl of, Lord-Lieutenant of Devon, 30, 36, 44, 55
beacons, 10, 21
Beceril, Juan, soldier, 64
Benson, E.F, biographer of Drake, 70
Bermudez, Juan, ensign, 64, 71–2
Bernardino, 102
Berry Pomeroy, Devon, 44
Bertendona, Martín de, commander of Levant squadron, 93
Biscay, Bay of, 5
Biscayan ship, 11, 15–16
Biscayan squadron, 5, 16
Bitus, Thomas, Irish priest, 78
Blake, William, 57
Blavet, Brittany, 57
Bodenham, Jonas, 85
Bonner, John, pilot, 74, 78
Boret, Jaque, mariner, of Olone, 102
Brady, Jacob, Irish priest with Armada hospital, 74
Bridewell, *see* Exeter or London
Brierly, *see* Burley
Brittany, 49, 57
Browne, Sir William, adventurer, 68, 78
Bruones, Anthonio de, 101
Brussels, 84–6
Burcia, Alonso de, 101
Burghley, Lord Treasurer, 47, 57, 86
Burgos, Diego Flores de Valdés imprisoned in, 92
Burley, Richard, *entretenido*, 74-6, 78

Cabrera, Juan de, boy, 102
Cabrito, Pedro Martín, soldier, 32, 40, 64, 67, 69
Cadiz, Andalusia, 6–8, 22, 30
Calais, Picardy, 4, 53, 71, 79, 85, 91, 93
Calderon, Juan, pothecary's assistant, 101, 104
Calderon, Pedro Coco, 12, 14
Calderon, Rodriguo de, hospital administrator, 100

INDEX

Callo, Luis, mariner, of Brest, 102
Calvo, Eliano, financier, 89
Camiles, Pedro, 102
Campos, Diego de, 29, 64, 66, 72, 74
Candelas, Juan de, 101
Candelas, Mathias de, 101
Cano, Bartolome, sergeant, 56, 100
Cap Blanc, Piere de, mariner, of
  Bayonne, 102
Caravallo, Gaspar, 102
Cardona, Don Juan de, 90
Carey, Sir George, 75
Caribbean, 6;
  English piracy in, 2
Carmona, Diego de, soldier, 64
Carpenter, A.C., 29
Carrera de las indias, 6
Cary, George, of Cockington,
  deputy-lieutenant of Devon, 18,
  22, 27–30, 32–5, 43–6, 48–53, 55,
  58–9, 74, 103
Cary of Clovelly, 59
Casa de Paz Grande, 5, 60–1, 104
Cascais, Portugal, 28
Castilla, Juan de, 101
Castillo, Gonzalo del, adventurer, 53,
  57, 83, 100;
    Luis del, his brother,
      adventurer, 100
Castra, Juan de, 102
Castro, Alvaro de, auditor's
  clerk, 100
Catalonia, 68
Cecil, Sir Robert, 86
Cely, Thomas, 63–4
Champernown, Richard, 38
Chance, pinnace, 27, 39
Channel, English, 2–4, 37, 79, 90–1
Chapman, Christopher,
  shipcarpenter, 36
Chatham, Kent, 28, 36–37
Clas, Cornelis, Dutch mariner, 102
clergymen, on Armada, 3, 9, 74, 103
clerical staff, on Armada, 3
Cockington, Devon, 44–5
Compañias sueltas, 9
Conde, Juan, 102
Corbett, Julian, 18
Cornwall, Armada sighted off, 2
Corro, Diego del, 101
Cortesio, Alonso, of Marcia, 101
Corunna, Galicia, 3, 5, 9–10, 22, 28,
  32, 51, 56, 67–8, 81, 104
Courtenay, Sir William, deputy
  lieutenant of Devon, 48–50, 52–3,
  56-8, 100

Crete, wine from, 32
Cuba, Valdés governor of, 87
Cubiaur, Pedro, 55–8, 61

Dallox *see* d'Aler
Daniel, Robert, entretenido, 78
Dart estuary, Devon, plate 7
Dartmouth, Devon, 18, 22, 25,
  27–30, 35–6, 44–5, 57, 86, 98
David, hulk, 5, 69
Delgado, Martín, 102
Deloney, Thomas, writer of
  ballads, 5, 69–70, 77, 97
Dennys (or Dennis), Sir Thomas, 34,
  52, 55
Deptford, Kent, 36
Desma (or Dezima), Francisco de la,
  hospital caterer, 54, 60, 100, 103–4
Devon, 18, 43, 49, 63;
  earldom of, 49;
  map of South Devon,
    frontispiece
Dias, Alonso, 102
Dias, Cosme, servant to Pedro
  Samillon, 102
Dieppe, Normandy, 84
Diez, Hernando, 101
Diez, Symon, of Arazena, 101
Dionisio, Irish adventurer, 78
Domingo, 102, 104
Domingues, Alonso, 101
Domingues, Bartholomeo, 101
Don Pedro, *see* Valdés
Dorado, Pedro, mariner, of
  Galicia, 102
Dover, Kent, 4, 35, 71, 91
Drake, Sir Francis, apparent
  friendship with Valdés, 92;
  buys armour from *Rosario*, 31;
  buys London house, 35;
  capture of *Rosario* and surrender
    of Don Pedro to, 1–2, 11–18,
    43, 63, 74–5, 91, 96;
  fate of money taken by *Rosario*,
    24–6, 34–5, plate 3;
  hated by Spaniards, 67;
  myth of, 2, 70, 93–4;
  his Portugal expedition, 28, 36,
    53–4, 58;
  raid on Cadiz, 6;
  Valdés his prisoner, 79–85;
  wife of, 82;
  widow of, 58
Drake, Richard, 24, 35, 79, 81–2,
  85–6, plate 9;
  Robert, 85

INDEX

Dunkirk, Flanders, 55
Duquesa Santa Ana, 8
Dutch prisoners, from *San Pedro*, 56
Dutch ships, blockading, 4

'Earland, Viscount of', 68
East Anglia, 2
Edgecombe, Peter, 38
Edward, Irish priest with Armada hospital, 74
Eijha, Andalusia, 64
Elizabeth I, 28, 31, 34–5, 44, 52, 54–5, 57, 70, 79, 81, 83–4, 86, 95
Elizabeth Drake, 63
Elliot-Drake, Lady Elizabeth, 26
England, 2–4, 7–9, 28, 48, 66–7, 70, 75–6, 80, 84, 87, 91
English fleet, 4, 15, 79, 81
English merchants, 58
English prisoners in Spain, 64
Englishmen, on Armada, 9, 20, 63, 67–8, 74–5, 81
Entretenidos, see unattached officers
Esher, Surrey, 10, 81–4
Estefono, Paolo, ship's boy, of Aragosa, 103
Estrade, Pedro, 14
Exe estuary, Devon, 49
Exeter, Devon, 57, plate 6;
    Bridewell, 44–5, 50, 60;
    town prison, 44, 60

Ferez, Francisco de, 101, 104
Fernandes, Domingo, cook, 101, 104
Fernandez, Juan, boy, 102
Fernandez, Martín, 102
Fernandez, Martín de, 102
Ferrol, Galicia, 56, 74
Ffoulkes, C.J., 31
Fitzmorris, Sir James, 68
Flanders, 2, 68, 74, 76, 87, 96;
    Army of, 2, 4, 23, 76;
    coastal defences of, 87
fleet, English, 4
Fleet, river, 64
Fleming, Captain Thomas, 47
Flemish prisoners, from *San Pedro*, 51;
    from *San Salvador*, 47–8, 52
Flemish soldiers, 95
Florentine galleon, 3
Florez, Pedro de, 101
Fortescue, Hugh, 38
Founes, Captain, 27

France, 56–7;
    possible help for Armada from, 68
Francisco, 102
Frenchmen, from *San Pedro*, 51, 56;
    from *San Salvador*, 47–8, 52
Fries, Mateo de, soldier, 64, 68
Frobisher, Martin, 34

Gago, Juan, mariner, of Galicia, 102
Gaietan, Juan, sergeant, 13, 15, 23, 25, 64–5, 74–5
Galicia, 6
galleys, 3, 6, 12, 69
galleasses, 3, 6
Garcia, Alonso, surgeon's assistant, 101, 103–4
Garcia, Blas, 101
Garcia, Francisco, 101
Garcia, Matheo, boy, 102
Garcia, Pedro, 101, 103
Garcia, Pedro, 102–3
Gateras, Bernardino, 102
Gendi, Jean, mariner, of Morbeau, 102
gentlemen adventurers, 3, 9, 74
George, boy, 102
Geraldine, Sir Gerald, *entretenido*, 68, 78;
    Sir Maurice, *entretenido*, 78;
    Sir Thomas, *entretenido*, 78
German gunner on *San Salvador*, 46
German merchant ships, 17
German soldiers, 95
Gijon, Asturias, 87
Gilbert, Sir John, of Greenway, deputy-lieutenant of Devon, 18, 22, 28–9, 32–6, 38, 43–6, 48, 50, 52, 103
Ginez, Brother, nurse, 101, 103
Golasia, Chrístoval de, 102
Golden Hind, bark, 47
Golden Hind, 37
Gomez, Thomas, nurse, 101, 105
Góngora, Bernardo de, Dominican friar, 13–14
Góngora, doctor of physic, 64, 66–9, 72, 93, 104
Gonzal, pilot, 102
Gonzales, Juan, nurse and barber, 101, 103
Gonzales, Juan, 102
Gorges, Tristram, 63, 80
Granado, Andreas, 102
Gravelines, battle of, 79
Greene, Robert, poet, 38, 92

INDEX

Greenway, Devon, 45
Grenville, Sir Richard, 75
Griego, Antonio, 56
Groyne, *see* Corunna
Guevas, Pedro de las, hospital steward, 100, 103–4
Guipuzcoan squadron, 10
Guise, Duke of, 68
gunnery officers, 3
guns, Spanish, 2, 8, 19, 22, 29, 69, 95;
    on *Rosario*, 19, 23, 26–30, 35–6, 39, 91, 98;
    English, 95

Hakluyt, Richard, 25, 94–6
Hanseatic League, 35
Hanson, Cornelis, Dutch ship's boy, 102
Haray, Francois, mariner of Bluet, 102
Harris, Christopher, 38, 103
Harsang, Jean de, interpreter and steward, 102
Hawkins, Sir John, 3, 5, 28, 47
Hawkins, John, shipcarpenter, 36
Hawkins, William, mayor of Plymouth, 28, 36, 41, 46
Hawley, Francis, JP, of Weymouth, 47–8
Hector, Doctor, 72, 74
Henry VIII, 49
Herdiz, Jacob, mariner, of Amsterdam, 102
Hernandes, Francisco, 101;
Hernandez, Anthonio, of Outrera, 101
    Diego, 101
    Gonzalo, 102;
        Juan, mariner, of Galicia, 102;
        Pedro, corporal, 100;
        Pedro, 101;
        Pedro, of Casorla, 101
Heywood, Thomas, playwright, 92
Hidalgo, Juan, 101
Hoby, Sir Edward, 72
Hoffeman, Hanse, mariner, of Hamburg, 102
Hoffeman, Jacob, his brother, mariner, of Hamburg, 102
Holland, Spanish prisoners in, 84;
    States of, 55
Hope Cove, Devon, 48–9, 52, 100, plate 8
hospital staff, Spanish, 3, 9, 51, 74, 100–5

Howard, Charles Lord Howard of Effingham, English Lord Admiral, 4, 6, 12, 15, 24, 27, 29, 35, 47, 80, 91, 94;
    Lord Thomas, 47
Huerta, Juan de, Paymaster-General, 14, 23–4, 47
Hughes, George, 24, 34
hulks, 3, 7, 12, 17, 69

Ilton 'Castle', Devon, 49–50, 53
Indies Guard galleons, 3, 7, 73
Ireland, 68, 76, 93;
    English soldiers in, 49;
    George Cary, future Lord Deputy of, 59;
    men from *San Pedro* in, 48–9;
    prisoners from, 72–3, 83–4
Irishmen, on Armada, 9, 20, 74
Italians, from *San Pedro*, 56

Jerez, Andalusia, 80;
    wine from, 32
Jheronimo, 102
Juannes, Anthonio, 101
Jusepe, mariner, of Genoa, 103

Kent, 4
Kinford, Patrick, *entretenido*, 78
Kingsbridge, Devon, 50, 53, 77
Kingston, Hampshire, 63–4

La Hogue, Normandy, 5
Laja, Galicia, 80
Lake, Henry, 31
Lario, Robert, *entretenido*, 78
Lasso, Don Rodrigo, 84
Latham, Captain, 58
Laughton, John Knox, historian, 51, 65
Le Havre, Normandy, 84
legal staff, on Armada, 3
Leicester, galleon, 17
Leon, Crístobal de, ancient bearer, 64
Leon, Pedro de, army captain, 9, 13, 64, 88
Lewis, Michael, 27
Leyva, Don Alonso de, 6, 10, 51, 66, 93, 100
Lifield, Mr, JP of Esher, 82
Lisbon, Portugal, 2–3, 6, 22, 30, 32, 65–7, 69, 104

Lisbon Muster, 3, 5, 9, 20, 51, 69, 74–5, 78
London, 4, 25–8, 36, 50, 53–5, 63, 66–7, 71, 73, 75, 80, 82–3;
  Billingsgate, 85;
  Bridewell, 58, 64–5, 72–4, 77, 80;
  City merchants, 53;
  The Herbar, Dowgate, 35, 82;
  Lord Mayor of, 64–5, 85;
  Marshalsea prison, 76;
  Newgate prison, 75;
  Paul's Cross, 26;
  St James Park, 82;
  St Paul's, 26;
  Steelyard, 35;
  Tower of, 28, 31, 75, 81
Lopez, Bartolomeo, 102;
  Doctor, 60, 72
Low Countries, *see* Netherlands
Lucerna, Antonio Rodriguez de, 56
Luscombe, Hugh, 34
Luzon, Don Alonso de, 84, 87
Lyassale, Ralph (or Raphael Sal), adventurer, 68, 78

Madre de Deus, 86
Maltby, 95
Mandurdeau, Lawrence, mariner, of Poitou, 102
Margaret and John, 13–17, 34, 53, 72
Marlborough, parish of, Devon, 49, 53
Marley, Sir Peter, *entretenido*, 78
Marlowe, Christopher, playwright, 92
Martin, Colin, 15, 91
Martín, Chrístoval, 101;
  Domingo, nurse, 101, 104;
  Gregorio, 102;
  Pedro, 101;
  Pedro, of Galerosa, 101
Martínez, Diego, hospital caterer, 100, 103–4;
  Juan, hospital chaplain, 100, 103–4
Mattingly, Garrett, 15–16, 91–2
Medina, Francisco de, wardrobe-keeper, 100, 103–4
Medina, Juan Gomez de, commander of squadron of hulks, 93
Medina Sidonia, Duke of, Captain general of Ocean Sea, 2–4, 8, 10–16, 23, 25–6, 47, 66, 70, 75, 80–1, 91–3;
  servants of, 3, 51

Mendoza, Bernardino de, 29, 49, 73, 80;
  Rodriguez de, 72;
  Vasco de Mendoza y Silva, army captain, 9, 53, 80–1, 83, 85, 89
Meque, Domingo de, 101
Mercoeur, Duke of, 56–7
Meredith, William, 89
Messia, Marco Antonio, 9, 70, 72–3
Mexia, Don Agustin de, *tercio* of, 9
Michael, Henry, *entretenido*, 78
Mighelson, Adrian, mariner, of Westfalia, 102
Minion of Plymouth, 31
Molma, Jheronimo de, 101
Moncada, Don Hugo de, 93
Mondragon, Gaspar de, 101
Moody, 83
Muñoz, Alonso de, sergeant, 100

Naish, George, 94
Naples, Italy, galleasses from, 3
Napoleonic wars, 94
Navarro, Brother, 104
Navy, British, 70, 94
Netherlands, 2, 54, 73, 100;
  English prisoners in, 65;
  history of war in, 93;
  Stanley's regiment in, 76
Nietto, Balthazar, of Merida, 101
Nivero, Ferdinando, mariner, of Galicia, 102
Norris, Sir John, 28, 35–6, 53–4, 58, 82
Norway, Armada wrecks on, 95
Noue, Francois de la, 84
Noue, Odet de la, seigneur de Teligny, 84
Nuestra Señora del Rosario, *see* Rosario
Nuñez, Gregorio, mariner, of Galicia, 102

O'Connor, Sir Charles, *entretenido*, 78
O'Dor, James, *entretenido*, 78
Oppenheim, M., 37
Oquendo, Miguel de, commander of Guipuzcoan squadron, 12, 93
Ortelio, Juan d', 101
Osely, Nicholas, 58
Owen, Evan, of Esher, 13, 15, 24, 35, 82
Oya, Domingo de, mariner, of Galicia, 102, 104

INDEX

Pagett, Sir Charles, 68
Palavicino, Sir Horatio, 72, 82–3
Pano, Salvador, 102
Pardo, Don Sancho, 64, 67, 74
Parma, Duke of, 4, 46, 54–5, 66, 68, 73–4, 79, 81, 84, 91, 96
pataches, 6
Pelegrin, Joseph, sergeant, 64, 68
Penmarque, Jean Luis de, mariner, 102
Peot, Vincent, mariner, of Morbeau, 102
Percyvall, Richard, scholar and translator, 83–5
Pereda, Don Melchor de, 47
Perez, Alonso, sexton, 102–3
Perez, Martín de, 101
Philip II, 2, 4, 6, 9–10, 15, 25, 29, 49, 55–8, 68, 73–4, 76, 80–4, 86–7, 90–2;
    sees Armada as crusade, 93
Pickford, Henry, 74, 78
pilots, 74–5, 81
Pimentel, 87
Pine, John, engraver, 25, 31
pinnaces, 69
Plymouth, Devon, 10, 28, 31, 36, 46, 49, 54–5, 57, 66, 81
Pole, Juan de, mariner, of Brest, 102
Portalegre, Count of, 59
Portsmouth, Hampshire, 35, 48, 64
Portugal, Viceroy of, 68
Portugal expedition, 28, 36, 53–4, 58
Portuguese prisoners, 53, 56, 58, 73;
    sailors, 73;
    ships, 3;
    soldiers, 51
Portland, Dorset, 27
Powderham, Devon, 49
Preto, Anthonio, 102
Privy Council, 22, 25–30, 32–6, 43–6, 48–53, 55, 58, 65, 70–1, 75–6, 80, 83, 85–6

Raleigh, Sir Walter, 2, 13, 38, 53, 72, 75
ransoms, 53–7, 73, 83, 85–7
Rata Encoronada, 68
Ratcliff, Mr, Alderman of the City of London, 65, 72
Recalde, Don Juan Martínez de, 11, 13, 15, 93, 100
Remes, Foulker, Dutch mariner, 102
Remes, Mighel, gunner?, of Hamburg, 102

Revenge, 11, 18, 24, 35, 43–4, 63, 79–80, 96
Ribadeo, Galicia, 6
Ribera, Luis de, ancient bearer, 25, 64
Richard of Dartmouth, 28
Riford, Robert, *entretenido*, 78
Rio, Gonzalo del, 102
Rivadavia, Galicia, wine from, 32
Robledo, Pedro, 53–4, 60, 105
Rodrigues, Anthonio, 101;
    Anthonio de, 101;
    Damean, 102;
    Juan, nurse, 101, 103–4;
    Luis, 102
Roebuck, 18, 26–7, 32, 39, 41
Rosario, bed from, 26, plate 4;
    capture and surrender, 1–2, 4, 10–18, 43, 53, 79, 82, 90–3, plate 1;
    crew of, 9, 43, 45, 91, 104;
    damage to, 10–17;
    embargoed, 6–7;
    expenses at Torbay, 35;
    flags from, 26, 38;
    goods from, 22–6, 28–9, 31–4, 44, 46, 49–50, 70;
    guns, armour and munitions on board, 23, 28–31, 36, 96;
    heavily armed, 8;
    inventory of, 22–3, 30, 35, 44, 98–9, plate 2;
    money on board, 2, 8, 20, 23–5, 34–5, 81;
    moved to Chatham, 36–7;
    pilot of, 74–5;
    prisoners from, 71–4;
    safe in Corunna, 9;
    soldiers on, 9, 30;
    tonnage, 6
Ross, ? Co Mayo, 48–9, 60
rowers, for galleys and galleasses, 3
Ruis, Anthonio, 102;
    Diego de, 101;
    Francisco de, 101;
    Juan, 102;
    Pedro, 102
Ruiz (or Ruys), Lopez, surgeon and chief pothecary, 53, 58–9, 60, 100, 103
Ryan, Sir Henry, *entretenido*, 78
Rye, Sussex, 80, 88

Sa, Anthonio de, 102
Salcombe, Devon, 49, 100
Sales, Bartholomeo de, 101

Salorzano, Juan Gonsalves, captain of galleass *San Lorenzo*, 72–3
Salvateria, Diego de, ensign, 100
Samaritan of Dartmouth, 27, 30, 39
Samillan, Pedro de, overseer of hospital, 49, 53–4, 60, 100, 102–4
San Felipe, 36
San Juan de Portugal, 11
San Lorenzo, galleass, 53–4, 71–3, 79
San Marcos, 14, 104
San Martín, Armada flagship, 12–14, 16, 24–5, 51
San Mateo, 68, 78, 88
San Medel, 56
San Nicolas Prodaneli, 48–9
San Pedro Mayor, 33, 104;
    prisoners from, 43, 50–3, 56–9, 100–5;
    wreck of, 48–54
San Salvador, explosion on, 10–12, 14–17, 24, 46–7, 95;
    goods from, 50;
    powder and shot from, 30;
    prisoners from, 43, 47, 51–2;
    sunk, 35;
    surgeon assigned to, 105;
    woman survivor from, 95;
    survivors from on *San Pedro*, 100–3
San Sebastian, Guipuzcoa, 75
Sandwich, Kent, 4
Santa Catalina, 16
Santa María, port, Andalusia, 64
Santander, 90
Santiago, soldier, 64
Santiago (Castille squadron), 78
Savales, Juan de, of Tordesillas, 101
Scilly Isles, 10
Scotland, 48
Semper, Sir William, 68
Serano, Juan, 102
Serna, Alonso de la, *entretenido*, 25, 40, 64, 66, 68, 71, 73
Seton, Richard, *entretenido*, 78
Seymour, Lord Edward, 32, 44
Shakespeare, William, 92
Sicily, 3;
    tercio of, 9
Silva, *see* Mendoza
Silva, Francisco de, captain of *San Pedro*, 100
Sneper, Henric, Dutch mariner, 102
Soliez, Diego, page to Don Alonso de Leyva, 51, 100
Solina, Gregorio, mariner, of Galicia, 102

Solorzano, *see* Salorzano
Sotomayor, Gregorio de, royal constable, 64–5, 67, 69, 73, 93
Spain, 2–4, 49, 51–2, 54, 56, 70, 72, 75–6, 84–5, 87;
    Armada returns to, 92–3;
    English prisoners in, 54, 65;
    merchants trading with, 46
'Spanish Barn', Torre Abbey, 44, plate 5
Stacey, Edmund, *entretenido*, 78
Stacey, William, *entretenido*, 75, 78
Standish, John, 85
Staveley, Sir William, 68
Stiago, Diego, of Cassalia, 101
Stone, Richard, 76
Strada, Andreas de, 101
Studland Bay, Dorset, 35, 48, 56
Stukely, William, 74
Sugero, Martín de, mariner, 102
Sulasar, Pedro, 102

Taguada, Gregorio de, chief nurse, 100, 105
Teligny, *see* Noue
Thames, river, 4, 35, 64, 66–7
Thanksgiving, sermon, 26;
    service, 26
Throckmorton Plot, 49
Tixeda, Jironimo de, 72
Toledo, Don Ferdinando de, *tercio* of, 100
Tolo, Bartolomeo de, 102
Tomson, Richard, 53–5, 71–2, 82
Torbay, Devon, 18, 25, 27, 29, 35, 43, 44
Torre, Geronimo de la, 13, 15
Torre Abbey, Devon, 44
Trenchard, George, vice-admiral of Dorset, 47–8

Ubaldino, Petruccio, 17–18, 46, 70, 90–1, 93–6
unattached officers, 3, 9, 74
Urcas, *see* hulks

Valdés, Diego Flores de, 13, 92–3
Valdés, Don Pedro de, commander of Andalusian squadron, and its flagship *Rosario*, 1, 8–10, 23–4, 75;
    account of loss of *Rosario*, 10–18;
    at Esher, 81–5;
    exchange with Winter, 84–6;
    goes home, 74, 87;

gatherer of intelligence, 20;
goods from, embezzlement
  of, 23–4, 33;
gunnery theories of, 8;
in Flanders, 87;
interrogation of, 70, 80–1;
negotiations for ransoms, 53–4;
on *Revenge*, 63, 79–80;
possibly gives Drake
  information, 2, 91–2, 94, 96;
returns from Indies, 6;
sent ashore, 79;
servants of, 9;
surrenders, 43;
valuables on board, 25–6
Van Meteren, Emanuel, 94
Vanegas, Alonso de, 12, 14, 25
Varaguan Jheronimo de, 101
Vazquez, Alonso, sergeant, 25, 40, 64, 67–8, 74, 93
Vega, Antonio de, 36
Venice, ambassador of in Spain, 56;
  Doge of, 56
Viana, *see* Viono
Victory, 41, 47
Victory (Nelson's flagship), 37
Viono, Juan de, master of
  Rosario, 30, 64, 67, 75

Wackelin, William, 71
Walsingham, Sir Francis, Principal
  Secretary of State, 6, 14, 18, 22, 29, 30, 32, 44–5, 54–5, 58, 72, 74, 80, 82–3
war, declaration of by Spain, 66
West Country, 26, 53, 56, 59, 64, 73, 82
Westmorland, Earl of, 68
Weymouth (Melcombe Regis),
  Dorset, 35, 47–8, 75;
    mayor of, 29

Whiddon, Jacob, 18, 26–7, 28, 30
whips, 69–70
Wight, Isle of, 29, 81, 91
Williamson, Jacob, mariner, of
  Amsterdam, 102
Winslade, Tristram, *entretenido*, 75–6, 78
Winter, Edward, exchange with
  Valdés, 84–6
Wood, Simon, 17, 82;
  Thomas, 37

Xanches, Chrístoval de, 101, 104;
  Diego, cook, 101;
  Martín, of Galerosa, 101;
  Pedro de, 102;
  Silvestre, of Marchena, 101
Ximenes, Andreas, 101;
  Ferdinando, 101;
  Francisco, 101
  Francisco de, 101;
  Juan, 101;
  Martin, pothecary's assistant, 100, 104

Yerua, Bartholomeo de la, assistant
  hospital caterer and sexton, 101, 103–4
Younge, Justice, 75
Ysidro, Geonese gunner, 56

zabras, 6
Zafra, Estremadura, 64
Zalzacer, Feriez de, 72
Zayas, Alonso de, army captain, 9, 53, 64, 80–1, 83, 85, 89
Zayas, Gabriel de, 84, 89
Zealand, Admiral of, 55
Zúñiga, galleass, 12